The Left Case for Brexit

Active government for an independent UK

Philip B. Whyman

CIVITAS

First published September 2018

© Civitas 2018
55 Tufton Street
London SW1P 3QL

email: books@civitas.org.uk

ISBN 978-1-906837-96-9

Independence: Civitas: Institute for the Study of Civil Society is a registered educational charity (No. 1085494) and a company limited by guarantee (No. 04023541). Civitas is financed from a variety of private sources to avoid over-reliance on any single or small group of donors.

All the Institute's publications seek to further its objective of promoting the advancement of learning. The views expressed are those of the authors, not of the Institute.

Typeset by
Typetechnique

Printed in Great Britain by
4edge Limited

The Left Case for Brexit

Contents

Author

Philip B. Whyman is Professor of Economics and Director of the Lancashire Institute for Economic and Business Research (LIEBR) at the University of Central Lancashire (Preston).

Phil has written on the economic relationship between the UK and the EU for more than two decades. Of his fourteen books on the topic, the most recent are: *The Economics of Brexit*, co-written with Dr. Alina Petrescu and published by Palgrave in 2017, and *Rethinking Economic and Monetary Union in Europe: A post-Keynesian alternative*, published by Routledge in 2018.

Before taking up his current university post, Phil spent time at the Bradford and Stockholm Universities – the latter through a Swedish Institute research fellowship. He additionally worked in the Economic and Research Department of USDAW as an economic researcher and European officer, representing the union on European matters at the TUC.

Acknowledgements

I am grateful for the insightful comments made on earlier drafts by Doug Nicholls, David Green and Daniel Bentley. The views expressed are my own and any errors or omissions are mine alone.

Abbreviations

acquis ommunautaire	The accumulated body of EU law and obligations from 1958 to the present day. It derives from international treaties, directives, regulations and judgements of the European Court of Justice. All new EU member states are obliged to accept all the existing aquis, whether immediately or after an initial transition period. Where there is a conflict, *aquis* take precedence over national law.
Brexit	The popular term used to describe the UK's withdrawal from the European Union.
CBI	Confederation of British Industry – the peak level business organisation in the UK.
CETA	The free trade agreement negotiated between the EU and Canada.
CHIEF	Customs Handling of Import and Export Freight – this is the IT system of the HMRC. It manages the declaration and movement of goods in and out of the UK, and collect revenue due to the state related to these movements. Importers, exporters and freight handlers can complete customs information electronically. Risk assessment is utilised to target physical checks of goods consignments, thereby providing low-risk trade faster passage.
CU	Customs Union – a trade bloc where members have agreed a FTA combined with a common external tariff. Customs unions typically also include a common external trade policy (where the CU has the monopoly right to negotiate trade deals on behalf of its members) together with commercial and/or competition policy.

ABBREVIATIONS

EEA   European Economic Area – comprises the EU member states and EFTA members Iceland, Liechtenstein and Norway. The EEA establishes something akin to the EU single market, in that it establishes the free movement of goods, services, capital and people, and participants are bound by the same rules and regulations as are established to regulate the EU single market.

EFTA   European Free Trade Association – an intergovernmental organisation, established in 1960, whose current member nations are Iceland, Liechtenstein, Norway and Switzerland. The UK was a founding member of EFTA but left in 1972 to join the EU.

EU   European Union – a political and economic union currently comprising 28 member states (27 once Brexit has been completed).

FCA   Facilitated Customs Arrangement – this is a term introduced in the 2018 UK government White Paper, which combines aspects of smart borders and customs partnership proposals. It outlines a suggested way in which the UK could act as if it were still in a customs union with the EU, through collecting EU tariffs on its behalf and introducing smart border technology to reduce trade friction.

FDI   Foreign Direct Investment – an investment made by a firm or person in one country into business interests in another country. This investment is 'active' in terms of retaining an element of control over business activity compared to more 'passive' overseas portfolio investment. FDI can occur through the take-over of an existing firm or through the establishment of a new entity; often described as 'greenfield' investment.

FTA   Free Trade Agreement

GDP   Gross Domestic Product – a measure of the market value of the output of goods and services produced within a specific time period.

Gig economy	The 'gig' economy is a popular expression referring to that section of the labour market characterised by temporary, short-term contracts or freelance jobs, as opposed to permanent, full time employment. Workers in the 'gig' sector often have more than one job. Hours can be irregular and insecure. Like musicians who travel from gig to gig, individuals working in the gig economy often perform separate pieces of work, for which they are paid separately, in the form of self-employed or temporary contractors.
IMF	International Monetary Fund – created in 1944 as part of the Bretton Woods post-war economic architecture, the IMF is intended to promote economic monetary cooperation, promote financial stability and facilitate international trade. It monitors the international monetary system and the financial policies of its 189 member nations, and thereby advises on potential risks to stability and appropriate policy adjustments. The IMF additionally provides loans to member nations experiencing actual or potential problems with their balance of payments, currency stabilisation or other structural problems undermining economic development and growth.
LSE	London School of Economics – a prestigious UK university and a constituent college of the federal University of London.
Max-Fac	Maximum facilitation – often described as max-fac or smart borders, involves the use of new technology driven solutions to ensure trade flows across borders.
MFN	Most Favoured Nation rules – whereby a nation agrees to treat all other nations no less advantageously than other nations. All WTO members agree to confer MFN status on each other. Exceptions are allowed for preferential treatment of developing nations and where preferential trade agreements (i.e. FTAs, customs unions) are negotiated.
NAFTA	North American Free Trade Agreement –a FTA creating a trade bloc between Canada, Mexico and the USA. It was established in 1994.

NIESR

National Institute of Economic and Social Research – founded in 1938, the NIESR is the UK's oldest independent economic research institute. The NIESR is independent of political attachment and is not affiliated to any single UK university, though its researchers work closely with different universities and it receives a significant proportion of its funding from research councils.

NTBs

Non-Tariff Barriers – whereas tariffs represent a tax on imports or exports between nation states, NTBs comprise any other types of measure that acts as a barrier or restraint upon international free trade. Examples may include quotas, administration compliance, rules of origin and other regulations which impact upon how a good can be produced and sold.

OBR

Established in 2010, the OBR is a non-departmental, statutory body created to provide independent economic forecasts and analysis of the public finances to be used in the preparation of the UK budget.

OECD

Organisation for Economic Co-operation and Development – founded in 1961, this intergovernmental organisation currently has 37 member nations, comprising the major high income market orientated economies. Originally founded to facilitate the Marshall Plan in the aftermath of the Second World War, it has built a reputation as a good source of statistics and economic analysis compiled for its member governments.

PEM

Pan-Euro-Mediterranean convention – participating nations agree to establish identical protocols with respect to rule of origin requirements, thus establishing mutual recognition of rule of origin statements across all participating nations. In addition, it allows materials originating in one participating nation to be used in the product of another participating nation without this invalidating the rule of origin requirements when exporting to a third participating nation.

PTA	Preferential Trade Agreement – where a group of countries agree to give preferential treatment to certain products. This may include FTAs or customs unions
R&D	Research and Development
Schengen area	The Schengen agreement is named after the small village in Luxembourg where it was signed. It enhances the freedom of movement of persons across those participating EU member states by abolishing border checks. Most EU member states have signed this accord, but not the UK, Cyprus, Ireland and Croatia. EEA membership involves acceptance of the Schengen agreement, so Iceland, Norway and Liechtenstein are part of the Schengen area, as indeed is Switzerland through its bilateral agreements with the EU. The Schengen agreement is currently experiencing difficulties following the 2015 terrorist attacks and the large numbers of migrants arriving at Europe's borders.[1]
SIM	Single Internal Market – this is more generally described as the EU 'single market'.
TFEU	Treaty on the Functioning of the European Union (TFEU) – together with the Treaty on European Union (TEU), the TEFU comprises the constitutional basis of the EU.
TUC	Trades Union Congress – the peak level federation representing the majority of trade unions in the UK.
UK	United Kingdom – made up of England, Scotland, Wales and Northern Ireland.
USDAW	Union of Shop, Distributive and Allied Workers.
White Paper	The UK government published a White Paper, in 2018, which outlined the principle features of a potential future trade relationship with the EU.
WTO	World Trade Organisation – an intergovernmental organization established in 1995, charged with regulating international trade. It replaced the General Agreement on Tariffs and Trade (GATT).

Foreword

The terms left and right are frequently used in political debate despite their lack of clear meaning. They don't even coincide with the positions taken by our main political parties.

The Labour party was once seen as the party of the left and the Conservative party of the right, but the mainstream Labour position favours EU membership, including support for its misnamed four freedoms, which are really the four axioms of market fundamentalism – free movement of goods, services, people and money – often seen as right wing. Moreover, mainstream Labour plays down the fact that immigration has driven down wages, especially among the lower paid, and disregards the fact that EU case law undermines the efforts of individual countries to protect living standards.

The European Court of Justice (ECJ) is no friend of trade unions. In two landmark cases in 2007, Viking and Laval, it put the interests of employers above those of rank and file workers. It used its powers to give the highest priority to the leading dogma of globalisation, namely that nothing should stand in the way of businesses that want to provide a service in another member state, even if their aim is to drive down pay and conditions.

Viking was a Finnish passenger ferry company that operated a vessel between Helsinki and Tallin, in Estonia.

It sailed under the Finnish flag and paid wages under a Finnish collective agreement. Viking tried to reflag to Estonia and pay lower wages. The European Court of Justice applied article 43 of the EC Treaty, which prohibits restrictions on 'freedom of establishment'. The effect of the ruling was to make the right to strike subordinate to the economic freedom of employers to relocate a business, even when plainly seeking a flag of convenience. Similar thinking was applied to Swedish building workers in the Laval case.

If to speak of the left means anything at all it must imply a commitment to active government for the benefit of everyone. To emphasise the good of everyone implies that an economic system could work only to the advantage of a few people. Several prominent voices in the Conservative party have attacked 'crony capitalism', including government ministers Jesse Norman and Michael Gove. The system, they say, has been rigged to benefit a select few. They want a legal framework that is to the advantage of everyone who works hard.

This publication by Professor Whyman is not aimed exclusively at members of any one political party. It appeals to people in all parties and none who want Britain to seize the opportunity of Brexit to renew our economy so that we all have a fighting chance of success.

The Chequers white paper declares support for EU law (deliberately misnamed a common rulebook) on goods, which means accepting prohibitions on state aid unless approved by Brussels. We urgently need to rebuild our economic life to make the most of Brexit and government investment in new productive capacity will be vital. Under the state aid rules we can expect rival EU companies to lobby Brussels to prevent us from out-competing them. This is the overriding reality of state aid rules: they allow existing vested interests to obstruct active government policies intended to increase the kind of prosperity in which all can share.

Professor Whyman's pamphlet demonstrates how active government policies could promote an economy that works for all.

David G. Green

Summary of the Main Argument

Brexit can be a positive event for the Left. Withdrawal from the European Union offers the potential for an active government to transform our economy for our mutual benefit. This, in turn, can reinvigorate our political debate, as new challenges and opportunities demand new and innovative solutions.

Unfortunately, too many on the Left overlook this potential. Too many of the proposals for Brexit are either ambiguous in key respects or too timid to provide a realistic plan to make the most of the UK's new independent status. As a result, they are likely to appeal to neither UK citizens nor EU negotiators.

What is needed is a clearer vision of how Brexit could be made to work for all communities across the UK. How Brexit can enable greater economic policy freedom of action and how this, in turn, can be used to transform the UK economy.

Long standing weaknesses in the UK economy need to be dealt with. These include issues relating to low levels of capital formation, poor productivity growth, a large and unsustainable trade deficit, problems with the efficient operation of the labour market and the need to rebuild manufacturing industry to rebalance the UK economy. New industries need to be nurtured in order to take advantage of the opportunities offered by Brexit, and which will, in turn, encourage the growth of more highly skilled jobs.

This requires a new and more imaginative use of economic

policy to deal with these problems. This should be founded upon an improved macroeconomic strategy which will better facilitate growth and investment. An active industrial policy is required to stimulate new manufacturing opportunities and thereby both enhance productivity growth whilst rebalancing the economy. An active labour market policy would aim to increase skill levels in the UK and resolve potential labour supply bottlenecks for key businesses as any new migration policy is introduced. The combination of these measures should lead to the creation of more highly skilled jobs, thereby facilitating the growth of a high performance, high wage economy.

The Brexit deal that the UK pursues with the EU, and which in turn will determine how it chooses to trade with the rest of the world, needs to assist and not hinder this economic transformation. It is therefore wrong-headed to start with discussing trade options with the EU and, having chosen a favoured approach, simply hoping that everything else will naturally fall into place. For the best possible Brexit solution to be achieved, the needs of the citizens and the economy have to take precedence, and only then should a trade deal be pursued with the EU that best meets these objectives.

Since the economic transformation that lies at the heart of a progressive Brexit solution is dependent upon the introduction of a more active range of economic policies in order to be successful, it is crucial that any preferred trade agreement with the EU does not unnecessarily constrain economic policy flexibility.

Viewed on this basis, the EEA (Norway) option is too restrictive, as it requires the UK to follow all EU rules and regulations pertaining to the single market, but without having any say in their design. Customs unions require the imposition of a common external tariff wall and commercial policy, meaning that the UK could not negotiate trade deals with other countries. It would probably also have to follow many of the same rules and regulations designed by the EU but over which the UK would have no input. Trading on the basis of World Trade Organisation (WTO) rules would allow maximum policy independence, within the ground rules set by WTO treaties, yet the introduction of tariff charges on many goods would be a cost to exporters that would be better avoided.

Therefore, the preferred trade relationship with the EU is for the negotiation of a free trade agreement (FTA). This seems to be the most advantageous of all trade options. It allows more policy independence than EEA and customs union options, thereby making it easier to achieve the economic transformation of the UK economy, yet it avoids most of the trade costs associated with the WTO option. Taking a parallel from a well-known children's story, where a small child tastes porridge made for three bears, if the EEA and customs unions are too hot, and the WTO option too cold, the FTA option comes closest to being just right.

The Left Case for Brexit would, therefore, propose the pursuit of a FTA with the EU, whilst simultaneously looking beyond our near neighbours in Europe to the trade and economic cooperation opportunities available across the rest of the globe. In order to take full advantage of these opportunities, and to ensure that as many UK citizens as possible share any resulting benefits, a Left Brexit should embrace the policy freedom arising from independence to pursue more active industrial, labour market and procurement policies. This would be further aided by a rejection of neo-liberal austerity and embracing a post-Keynesian macroeconomic framework capable of sustaining this more progressive economic model.

Introduction

It is now more than two years since the UK voted to withdraw from the European Union (EU) in the 2016 European referendum. In the aftermath of the vote, both of the two main political parties, Conservative and Labour, stated unequivocally that they accept the result (Conservative Party, 2017:1; Labour Party, 2017:24). The question of the UK leaving the EU would therefore appear to be settled, with those still advocating parliament to somehow frustrate the expressed desire of the British electorate appearing to be increasingly out of step with public opinion and their viewpoint unlikely to gain any significant traction.

Yet, two years on from the referendum, we have still not completed the Brexit process. Indeed, arguments are still ongoing about some pretty basic things, such as what sort of future relationship we would like to forge with the EU and the rest of the world. It is no wonder that probably most people, irrespective of how they voted, are bemused with the lack of progress. Most of us, I suspect, just wish that our political leaders would just get on with Brexit and stop dragging out the whole process.

Talk of transition deals is fine if the vision of what the UK is transitioning towards is clear. But it is not. As a consequence, the desire to agree transition periods appears more like putting off difficult decisions – so called 'kicking the can down the road'.

The most recent episode of political theatre, culminating in the Chequers agreement and resulting Cabinet resignations, just adds to the sense of confusion and timidity characterising too many of the proposals being made about Brexit. Confusion, because too many of the details in the various schemes are simply not workable or are unlikely to be palatable to those on the EU side of the negotiating table. Timid, because they demonstrate an undue focus upon the challenges which Brexit generates, without seeming to place sufficient weight on the opportunities that it simultaneously provides.

Such prevarication must be rejected. Brexit can be made to work for most people, so long as policy makers are far-sighted enough to use the new opportunities that independence brings to transform the economy and with it the prospects of all communities across the UK.

There will be those who are sceptical that this can happen. Many on the Left are concerned that Brexit may result in the UK becoming a less open and a nastier society. Others still cling to the vision of a social Europe, propounded by Jacques Delors to the TUC as long ago as 1988. They find it difficult to accept that this vision has never been properly realised and, indeed, over the past thirty years, the EU has shifted markedly in a neo-liberal direction.[1] If you share these concerns about Brexit, I simply ask you to keep an open mind until you have finished reading this pamphlet.

For others, who are more enthusiastic about the prospects following Brexit, but who are frustrated that much of the ideas and analysis on how to make Brexit work emerges from the Eurosceptic Right, I hope that I have provided you with a broad economic policy framework within which many of your hopes and expectations may be realised.

For parliamentarians, who have been given the difficult

job to navigate through the uncharted waters of Brexit, I hope what follows will provide you with food for thought and outlines a potential way forward to gain the maximum benefit for the country from this complicated process.

The important point to note is that Brexit is simply a means to an end – it is not the end in and of itself. At its heart, Brexit is no more and no less than the UK having taken a decision to do things differently than before. To take back control over certain aspects of its national life that a majority of its citizens have judged were being too heavily constrained by the rules and directives designed in Brussels.

The idea of 'taking back control' should have a natural appeal to many on the Left, since the democratic control over the levers of power in the economy are at the heart of many Fabian, democratic socialist, progressive green, left-liberal and social democratic schools of thought. The idea of taming the worst excesses of a free market system and creating an economy that benefits the many and not just the few is a founding principle of the Left.

But taking back control is not enough – the crucial thing is what we decide to do with this control. Brexit needs to be far more than a narrow exercise in engineering a break-up with the EU in such a way that we stay friends afterwards. So much attention has been devoted to this element of the withdrawal process, by both economists and politicians, that it sometimes seems difficult to raise our eyes and consider how Brexit may be a catalyst to envisioning a new way of doing things.

In the economic sphere, this requires a transformation of the economy to deal with current weaknesses in the UK economy. This is necessary to meet the challenges, and take advantage of the new opportunities, that will arise. These changes are long overdue and would need to happen at some point, Brexit or no Brexit. But independence from the EU will make these changes much easier to make.

The transformation of our economy requires a more active form of government. It will necessitate a more active industrial policy, aiming to rebuild our manufacturing sector by taking advantage of new products and new markets. It will benefit from an active labour market policy, designed to develop a more highly skilled labour force to prevent skills bottlenecks and hence meet the needs of the new high skill, high wage employment opportunities created. It would be aided by the use of public procurement to help to anchor prosperity in local and regional economies across the UK, thereby ensuring that all communities benefit from Brexit. And all of this needs to be facilitated by a more active form of macroeconomic policy, drawing inspiration from post-Keynesian rather than neo-liberal foundations, to maintain the momentum in transforming the UK economy.

The ultimate aim is to find a resolution to the type of Brexit that ensures that the economy is transformed and, in the process, benefits as many people in as many communities across the UK as possible. This ultimate goal should prove attractive to readers from all political persuasions or none. But the vision of using the policy freedoms, which are available from certain forms of Brexit, to create a more prosperous, fairer economy and society, should be of particular interest to those on the Left.

This is the task this pamphlet has set itself – to outline the principles of what changes need to be made to transform our economy for the benefit of all communities within the UK, and from that to consider which of the various Brexit options available to policy makers would be best to deliver these objectives.

1

What Would a Left Brexit Look Like?

A progressive or Left Brexit will be characterised by a number of key features. Firstly, it should benefit all communities across the UK. This is essential. If we are to move beyond the political divisions exposed during the referendum campaign, our future prosperity as an independent nation must benefit as many people as possible. Hence, Brexit must benefit workers as well as businesses. The countryside as well as urban areas. The north as well as the south. There should be no left-behind areas that do not share in the future prosperity of the nation.

This requires a genuine sharing of the costs and benefits that are likely to arise from the Brexit process itself and the resulting future prosperity of the UK economy. It is important, both for reasons of fairness and to create a shared vision for the future direction of the UK, that this time we really are all 'in it together'.

The creation of a stronger and more balanced economy should help to spread economic prosperity more evenly across the UK. This will be aided by a combination of industrial policy measures and skills development. A more productive economy will, in turn, facilitate better jobs and higher wages. However, where this does not prove to be sufficient, fiscal redistribution and additional regional policy measures will be required to ensure that there are no 'left behind' areas who do not benefit from post-Brexit economic growth. All communities should benefit. None should feel excluded.

Secondly, in order to ensure that the UK takes full advantages of the opportunities which will arise from its position as an independent nation, the economy needs to be transformed. Current economic weaknesses need to be dealt with. Policy makers need to consider how to best utilise the greater range of new and more innovative policy solutions that become available as an independent nation. This is necessary if we are to re-shape and re-balance the UK economy.

Tackling our economic weaknesses will necessitate fresh thinking on how to better promote greater productivity, sustainable economic growth and decent employment opportunities. It will require greater focus upon how to utilise an active industrial strategy to rebuild manufacturing industry and an active labour market strategy to equip our people for future needs and challenges. It will, additionally, help to reduce the very large trade deficit the UK has with the EU, and in the process reduce some of the drag upon UK growth potential.

Both of the main political parties recognise the importance of creating a strong economy that works for everyone. For the Conservatives, 'a strong economy is the basis for everything we want to achieve as a nation' (Conservative Party, 2017:13). Whereas for Labour, 'Britain needs to negotiate a Brexit deal that puts our economy and living standards first...creating an economy that works for all' (Labour Party, 2017:4,7). Yet, a similarity of goals does not necessarily make a consensus on how to move forwards.

My view is that it is vital, if these ambitions are to be

realised, that policy makers use the full range of policy tools available to them in order to create a truly successful and resilient economy. This is easier to accomplish in a more independent nation. Therefore, the choice of Brexit option has a role to play in the more progressive transformation of our society and economy. But to make Brexit count, we need to choose wisely.

2

Creating a Resilient Economy

Depending upon how comparable values of GDP are measured, the UK has the fifth or sixth largest economy in the world (IMF, 2018). We are a prosperous nation and will remain so whatever relationship we choose to have with the EU and other nations in the future.

Yet, this is not the whole picture. There are also a number of weaknesses that currently constrain our economic potential. The damaging effects arising from the economic uncertainty surrounding Brexit are an obvious issue that needs rapid and satisfactory resolution. Hopefully, as it will be shown, it is possible to establish an economic framework which will help to deal with much of this uncertainty. However, many of the other challenges to the UK economy are more fundamental and have been ignored for a number of years.

It is easy to overlook fundamental weaknesses in the economy during those periods when economic progress appears to be superficially fairly satisfactory. This is a lesson that every central banker and policy maker knows only too well – that the time to implement necessary change is very often when things look too good to be true, but that very fact often blinds most people to the need for change. However, the fallout from the 2008 global financial crisis, the subsequent period of austerity and the UK's pending withdrawal from the EU, have focused greater attention upon these issues.

Due to space considerations, I propose to focus upon five economic challenges facing the UK. These are:

1. the very large trade deficit the UK runs with the rest of the world (primarily the EU), which means that for some time, the UK has been living beyond its means in trade terms;

2. weak productivity growth that has characterised the UK economy over a long time period, but which has grown worse since the near stagnation following the onset of the 2008 financial crisis;

3. comparably low levels of gross capital formation – resolving this would assist in boosting productivity growth;

4. flaws in the labour market – an active labour market policy could help to resolve a number of consequences arising from a post-Brexit immigration policy, whilst enhancing the mutually beneficial aspects of a flexible labour market and dealing with some of the negative effects arising from casualization and insecurity in employment;

5. rebalancing the UK economy – one of the main policy tools to achieve this goal is through the development of an active industrial strategy.

These challenges for the UK economy exist irrespective of Brexit. Had the UK remained a full member of the EU, they would have needed tackling at some point. This would have been more difficult to achieve bound by the rules and regulations of the EU, but they would have needed facing up to eventually.

The key point here is that the additional challenges and opportunities created by Brexit should not be viewed in isolation. Too many economic studies do precisely this – using the economic maxim of holding everything else the same (*ceteris paribus*), they ignore or assume away other difficult issues. Yet, if we are considering how to re-imagine economic policy to deal with the impact of Brexit, this has to take into account all other challenges facing the economy at the same time.

Why? Well, Brexit is related to all of these issues. The trade deficit is the most obvious, where judicious trade policy could make significant inroads into our current inability to trade sufficiently to pay our way in the world. But policies aimed at boosting capital investment need to be considered alongside measures taken to reduce uncertainty over Brexit. Similarly, making greater use of the range of industrial policy measures after Brexit should help to reinvigorate manufacturing industry which, in turn, should contribute towards rebalancing the UK economy and facilitating productivity growth. The resulting demand for better, higher skilled jobs, should go some way towards eliminating the more damaging aspects of labour market flexibility.

If the challenges posed by Brexit – positive and negative – are viewed in this more holistic way, then it becomes clearer what sort of changes are needed to be made to strengthen the economy. It should, in turn, help to clarify which of the various options relating to future post-Brexit trade with the EU would be more helpful in turning the UK economy around.

Challenge One – Reducing the Trade Deficit

Taking these economic challenges in turn, the first has the most obvious relevance to Brexit, because the vast majority of the trade deficit that the UK currently faces relates to our trade with the EU. The trade deficit concerns the gap between what we sell abroad (exports) and what we as a nation buy from abroad (imports). Currently, the UK runs a £29bn trade deficit, which is composed of a trade deficit of £71.6bn with the EU and a surplus of £42.9bn with the rest of the world.[1] This has actually declined since the EU referendum, as the depreciation in sterling has provided a boost to exports. In 2015, the UK ran a trade deficit with the EU equivalent to 4.6% of its GDP (IMF, 2016), whereas this had declined somewhat to 3.5% at the end of 2017, although the very latest figures suggest that this gap may be widening once again.[2]

Why does this matter? Well for much the same reason as if you were persistently spending more than your income. The UK has been financing this trade deficit by a combination of borrowing, selling off assets and encouraging additional flows of capital into the UK. The latter can be good news, if this is in the form of 'greenfield' FDI investment, where new factories or service providers are set up in the UK and add to existing capacity. The balance of economic evidence is less clear cut, however, if this inflow of money is to take-over existing UK firms. New management might increase efficiency or it may asset strip existing value. It may provide a new source of valuable export activity for the UK economy, or it may frustrate the expected boost that normally comes from currency depreciation by increasing prices to maintain the value of overseas profits. The recent 'Marmite-gate' controversy would seem to be one such example of the latter effect.

There is a second effect, however, that is less visible but more damaging to the prosperity of the UK, namely that a persistent trade deficit can have a depressive effect upon UK growth rates (CEPG, 1979:28; Thirwall, 2011). In the simplest terms, if the UK eliminated its trade deficit with the EU by increasing exports to the value of what it currently imports, it would have an additional 3.5% (or around £70.8bn) of its national income to spend on a variety of projects. This could be used for a variety of different purposes, including increasing funding to the NHS and other public services, enhancing transport and infrastructure, or encouraging the expansion of the UK productive sector.

How might the UK eliminate this trade deficit? Well, there are two approaches. The first is the 'hair shirt' form of economics that would prioritise reducing imports by squeezing consumption and as a result causing the UK economy to shrink. This would reduce imports but at a substantial cost in terms of lost output and wasted human potential.

The second is to seek to increase exports. Part of this can be through striking favourable trade deals with other countries in order to sell more of what we currently produce.

A future trade arrangement with the EU would be a significant part of this, since the UK currently sells around 44% of its total exports to EU member states. For some, protecting this current trade is what is most important. For them, the most advantageous form of Brexit is one which limits any loss of trade with our largest single market, presumably through forming as close an association with the EU as possible (such as the EEA or perhaps a customs union) or alternatively remaining a full member of the organisation. This might involve the UK agreeing to implement whatever rules and regulations the EU decides to introduce. Essentially, this is the 'bird in the hand is worth two in the bush' type of argument.

However, this alone will not solve the trade deficit problem for two rather obvious reasons. Firstly, because the trade deficit with the EU has been persistent and increasing during our time as members of the organisation. Therefore, the act of remaining as close to full membership as possible will not, by itself, solve a problem that emerged during our period of membership. Part of this trade balance deterioration may be due to the fact that the EU single market is primarily focused on goods and is only patchy in terms of services, yet it is in the latter where the UK has a current competitive advantage.[3] A customs union would do little in this regard, since it is similarly focused on goods rather than services, whereas EEA or a FTA would fare better, but these options would still not, by themselves, be able to narrow the trade gap.

Secondly, those that argue for close alignment with the EU do so to minimise short term costs arising from potential loss of trade arising from an increase in the costs of carrying out this trade. However, this is only one side of the balance sheet. One of the potential advantages that Brexit brings is the ability for the UK to negotiate future trade relationships with other countries throughout the world. Even now, with our focus being upon the European market, the UK still sells 56% of its exports outside of the EU. Moreover, there is an expectation that a large majority of future global growth will occur outside of the EU (HMG, 2018:48).

The ability to explore future trading arrangements with non-EU nations should help to grow exports further, thereby improving the overall balance of trade. It is difficult to estimate the likely benefit that might flow from such possibilities, since most economic studies have not (to date at least) successfully modelled the likely result. Nevertheless, it is safe to surmise that there would be some additional gains to be made from any such new trade agreements, which would need to be balanced against maintaining existing trade links with the EU.

Customs unions do not allow members to negotiate their own trade deals with third parties, and therefore should the UK participate in a future customs union with the EU, it would make it more difficult to grow non-EU trade. Other Brexit options would therefore appear to have the edge on growing trade across the globe.

Advocates of the closest possible trade alignment with the EU might argue that there are other measures that could be used to boost trade irrespective of the relationship with the EU, and that is true. Maintaining a competitive exchange rate can assist in reducing the trade deficit by lowering the cost of UK goods denominated in sterling in foreign markets. The effectiveness of this policy has been witnessed since the fall in sterling following the European referendum, as exports have increased and import substitution has further reduced the trade deficit. The short term effect has not been as substantial as might have been anticipated, due to the tendency of a large number of firms preferring to bank this advantage as increased profits rather than use it to expand export sales (Takyi and D'Silva, 2017). Nevertheless, it is likely that a longer term managed currency strategy, combined with a more favourable macroeconomic policy aimed at reducing uncertainty and increasing business expectations of future profitable sales opportunities, would deliver a more sustained and favourable effect.

Yet this policy works equally well whatever form of Brexit is chosen – whether the UK is closely aligned with the EU or not. Indeed, it might be argued that the management of the exchange rate could offset all or part of any increase in trade costs that might flow from more independent forms of trade policy.

This is only part of the answer, however, because these solutions only focus on what the UK currently produces which, as evidenced by the size of the trade deficit as a whole, is simply insufficient. Trade deals alone can help to sell more of the same goods or services, but what is really required is for the UK to broaden its range of potential exports. Not just to increase output of existing product and service ranges, although that would be beneficial, but to make and sell different goods and offer new forms of services.

This can be done through encouraging additional firms to export – through use of business networks and dedicated support services to simplify the process for first time exporters. A wider range of firms might extend the UK export offer. But it also requires the broadening of the UK's productive base, in order to develop new products and related services, engage with new and growing markets (perhaps in battery technology, graphene or renewables) and generally grow the export-orientated segment of the economy.

This will require the maintenance of a macroeconomic policy which encourages production and innovation, combined with an active industrial strategy aimed at growing these necessary areas of the economy. These issues will be discussed in more detail under Challenge Five.

Dealing with the trade deficit, therefore, requires more than simply doing much of the same things after Brexit. Certainly, current trade links need to be nurtured. But new market opportunities must also be explored. Innovative products and services need to be developed and exported to take advantage of those opportunities created by Brexit. A more active economic policy framework needs to be introduced to facilitate this process. Therefore, the form of Brexit which will assist in resolving the trade deficit will be one which best enables all of these things to occur.

Challenge Two – Solving the UK's Productivity Problem

The UK has a productivity problem which needs addressing. UK productivity growth lags behind most of our leading competitors (see Figure 1). Compared to the USA, for example, UK output per person employed has remained pretty consistently between 25% and 30% lower, over a long period of time (Bank of England, 2015:48). Comparisons with the Euro area and OECD average are not as stark, but, when measured in terms of output per hour worked (the best measure of productivity), UK productivity is around one third weaker than that of France and Germany.[4]

Figure 1: International comparison of productivity measured via GDP per hour worked, selection of countries, 1990 – 2017, expressed in US dollars (constant prices 2010).

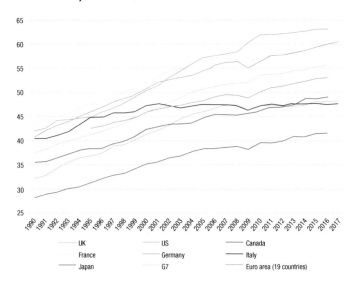

(Source: OECD, 2018).

The UK did appear to be narrowing this productivity gap with the Eurozone economies in the years immediately preceding the 2008 financial crisis. However, some of this may have been due to the bubble that was being created by the over-expansion of the financial sector; a bubble which subsequently and spectacularly burst. In the aftermath, since 2008, UK productivity has barely risen at all. Thus, UK productivity stagnation has led to the widening of the gap once more.

This represents a decade of wasted opportunities and, indeed, the worst performance since 1974 which was in the middle of the three day week! Had the UK registered even its pre-crisis performance over the past decade, productivity would have been more than 20% higher than today, with the resulting potential for higher wages, employment and growth (see Figure 2).

Figure 2: Output per hour and output per worker, UK, 1994 to 2017, seasonally adjusted

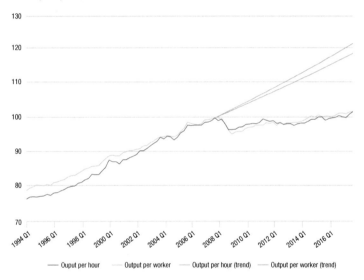

(Source: ONS, 2017dm).

This poor performance is, unfortunately, not a recent phenomenon. The UK has registered comparably poor productivity growth throughout most of the post-Second World War period, averaging slightly less than 1.3% per annum. Hence, this is a long term problem that requires fixing.

Why? Well, Nobel Prize winning economist Paul Krugman (1994:11) explains it rather well when he states that:

> Productivity isn't everything, but in the long run it is almost everything. A country's ability to improve its standard of living over time depends almost entirely on its ability to raise its output per worker.

Productivity is a major determinant of economic growth and hence higher wages. You can achieve economic growth by simply adding more inputs into a process – i.e. more of the same machines or more people, perhaps encouraged to work in the UK as migrant labour from the EU or elsewhere. But this is wasteful. Output and GDP may increase but GDP *per person* may very well not. Therefore, far better to achieve growth by becoming more efficient – i.e. producing more from a given amount of inputs.

This can be achieved by working smarter or, for short periods of time, increasing work intensification, although this latter does not work well as a long term strategy for obvious reasons. Increasing the skills composition of the workforce is important, as is innovation, the leadership skills and motivation of business leaders, the flexibility of the labour market, institutional factors such as the efficiency of the wage bargaining system or the regulation of industry and so forth. However, the largest contributor to productivity growth in the UK is capital investment (BIS, 2015b:58). After all, even highly skilled and educated individuals find it difficult to increase productivity if working with outdated machinery and IT equipment. Similarly, innovation is likely to be still-born without the necessary investment to embed it in production and make the new techniques flourish.

Given the range of potential determinants, it is important, when developing a productivity strategy, to create a bundle of mutually reinforcing interventions each providing support to businesses, employees and creating an economic framework within which innovation and growth can flourish. This can combine establishing support mechanisms for firms at local or regional level, to support their growth potential. It can include the re-examination of national institutional arrangements, such as for example, revisiting labour market flexibility to identify which elements work best to create mutual advantage for both firms and employees. It must also encourage more and smarter capital investment in the productive sector, if the UK is to meet its economic challenges.

The form of Brexit that will best facilitate efforts to address the UK's poor productivity challenge will be the one which best encourages investment, innovation, the development of new industries and market opportunities. It is unlikely that close alignment to current EU rules and regulations will assist this new strategy. Indeed, there is a good argument to suggest that national rather than EU regulations may better meet the needs of UK businesses and UK priorities.

Challenge Three – Stimulating Capital Formation

The UK typically lags behind other comparable countries in terms of the average rate of fixed capital formation, R&D expenditure and spending on higher education (skills) as a percentage of GDP.[5] Weak performance has persisted for decades (see Figure 3). This includes the whole period of EU membership. Thus, it is important to note that, whilst the uncertainty surround Brexit is not helpful, the problems underlying the UK's poor capital formation performance are more deep seated and will require more substantive policy corrections to address.

Figure 3: Gross capital formation[6] as % of GDP, selected countries, 1967-2016

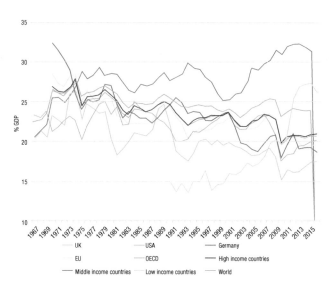

(Source: World Bank, 2016).

A low level of investment is bad for the economy for four main reasons. Firstly, as previously discussed, it represents the primary driver of productivity and hence growth in GDP and living standards. Secondly, investment underpins innovation – investment is needed to turn good ideas into action in order to generate material benefit. Thirdly, investment and innovation can transform the export potential of UK industry, increasing its efficiency and thereby having the potential to raise quality of reduce cost, and thereby stimulate sales. Finally, investment is a key component of aggregate demand in the economy and as such it is a key means of creating the favourable market conditions which will encourage further investment and an expansion of productive activity.

Raising capital formation, through spending on new plant, machinery and physical infrastructure (i.e. roads, hospitals, schools), benefits the whole of the UK. It encourages greater training and skills development for those working with the new and improved equipment, and by raising their productivity it creates the potential for higher wages in the future. For the same reasons, more productive and more highly skilled employment opportunities are likely to require better quality apprenticeships and encourage an expansion of vocational education and training to meet the needs of industry.

What is particularly chastening is that this dismal investment record has occurred despite a sharp increase in inequality levels within the UK. As national income has shifted from wages to capital, orthodox economic theory would have anticipated that productive investment would have been facilitated. Yet, the evidence suggests that lowering taxes upon entrepreneurs and capital holdings has not worked for the UK. Indeed, it would appear that rising inequality has depressed, rather than boosted, economic growth (Chang, 2010; OECD, 2014b). Tax cuts for the rich, to encourage investment in productive industries, does not seem to be a particularly effective policy solution.

Instead, the factors behind the UK's dismal investment record are more fundamental. Going back to basics, what has been lost in the dominance of supply-side orthodoxy in economic thinking, is the fact that businesses invest because they believe that they can sell what they produce at a profit. Whilst cost factors can influence this calculation to a minor extent, what actually drives business investment is *demand* and the *expectation* of favourable future trading conditions. If businesses are uncertain about the future, or if demand is not sufficient to sustain the growth in future sales, investment will be delayed or abandoned until circumstances are more favourable. At this fundamental level, businesses are all Keynesians.

This is why the uncertainty surrounding the eventual form of Brexit is potentially damaging to the UK economy. But this is only one element in the current unwillingness of business leaders to invest at a level where they would make a significant different to growth and productivity rates.

The UK's weak recent growth trajectory, prolonged unnecessarily in significant part to the consequences of austerity measures, has conditioned many business leaders to be overly cautious. Indeed, one consequence of this has been a disappointing reaction to the depreciation of sterling, with many businesses preferring to take the free gift of increased profits rather than take advantage of the opportunities to use their more competitive prices in order to pursue greater sales abroad.

To break through this overt caution, and to stimulate the expectations of more favourable market opportunities in the future, government needs to step in and provide a stimulus to demand. By ensuring a sufficient level of aggregate demand in the economy, government policy can encourage investment which will, in turn, promote further economic growth and productivity.

However, by itself, this is insufficient. Stimulating demand, without altering the structure of the UK economy, will draw in more imports and make the trade deficit worse. It may help to solve one of the challenges to the UK economy but at the cost of making another worse. There might, additionally, be inflationary consequences if demand is stimulated too rapidly, before the productive potential of the economy has expanded to sustain this higher level of activity. Hence, a supportive macroeconomic stance, aimed at increasing employment and investment, needs to be accompanied by an active labour market and industrial strategy.

The implication for the choice of Brexit strategy is therefore clear. Clarification of the model under which the UK will operate as an independent nation following withdrawal from the EU is required to eliminate the uncertainty frustrating business. In order for this new vision of an independent Britain to be sustainable, and therefore give firms the confidence to invest and plan for the future, it needs to address the weaknesses in the UK economy and generate new incentives for growth.

Active government can assist this process. Macroeconomic policy can ensure a sufficient level of aggregate demand in the economy to encourage producers to invest to expand, whilst the development of new products and innovation to be encouraged through an active industrial strategy will generate further optimism and business opportunities. The development of additional markets for UK exports will further encourage this self-reinforcing loop. Hence, the form of Brexit chosen needs to be able to encourage these positive developments.

Challenge Four – Resolving Weaknesses in the Labour Market

An important area where the rebalancing of the UK economy will have a significant impact will be in the labour market. On one level, this would appear to be functioning well, as unemployment failed to rise as predicted during the recession provoked by the 2008 financial crisis. This was ascribed, in large part, to the flexibility of the UK labour market. However, it has become clear that there are weakness in terms of poor productivity developments, which are not aided by insecurity and casualization in part of the flexible labour market. As a result, real wages have stagnated over the past decade. Indeed, between 2007 and 2015, the UK was the only large advanced economy in which wages contracted while the economy expanded, and the second worst performer in the whole of the OECD – the worst being Greece.[7] Depressed wage growth leads to weak consumer demand and hence acts as a drag to growth.

In addition, there is an expectation that Brexit will restrict the inward flow of migrant labour from the EU. If this occurs, it would require further policy action to enhance skills within the domestic workforce in order to meet the requirements of British businesses (CBI, 2016). Even a well-designed migration policy is likely to have problems resolving all skills-related capacity constraints in the economy, caused when certain types of skills are in relatively short supply. Moreover, it is difficult to apply any system of immigration control with sufficient flexibility to meet the needs of an ever-changing labour market.

These issues can be tackled by separate policy measures. However, it makes more sense to deal with all of them simultaneously through an active labour market policy. This could moderate any unintended effects of a new work permit system, whilst providing assistance to UK companies as they might seek to expand their internal training and/or apprenticeship schemes. Moreover, enhancing skills will also make a contribution to tackling productivity stagnation and create a new range of more secure and well paid jobs. Targeting skills development in certain sectors would additionally facilitate the operation of industrial policy.

But an active labour market policy is more than simply better education and training provision. It can help to better match of individuals to vacancies, whilst a judicious use of educational bursaries and/or expanding the use of enhanced apprenticeships should help to reduce potential skills bottlenecks in the medium term. The promotion of geographical mobility to ease labour market shortages in specific key sectors. Whilst, during periods of economic downturn, temporary public works could prevent unemployment from eroding the skills and work capability of those who would otherwise become unemployed.

Many of these measures seek to enhance the positive aspects of the UK's relatively flexible labour market (Siebert, 1997), whilst dealing with some of its negative consequences. If this can be achieved, flexible labour markets can secure mutual benefits for firms, workers and society (Whyman and Petrescu, 2014). But for this to occur, a degree of trust between participants is essential (Guest and Peccei, 2001). It won't work if flexibility is simply used to boost profits for some at the expense of the working conditions endured by others. High performance workplaces depend upon the trust and participation of a high skilled workforce (Michie and Sheehan-Quinn, 2001). Functional flexibility, in these circumstances, promotes high levels of productivity.

This is quite a different business model to that characterised by the self-employed and casualised segment of the labour market. For those amongst the estimated 6-14 million workforce who choose this type of work, there is obviously little problem. Flexibility, for them, makes it easier to balance work-life commitments.

It is significantly different, however, for the estimated one quarter to one third of this total who do not choose to undertake self-employment or casualised contracts (Manyika et al, 2016:4,8-9). Consequently, the expansion of high performance job opportunities, combined with the provision of skills training and quality apprenticeships, should measurably improve the circumstances of these individuals whilst delivering potential gains for the economy as a whole. Enabling the movement of individuals who are currently working in the casualised sector because of the dearth of real alternatives, towards more highly skilled occupations, and in the process helping to resolve skills shortages in certain areas, would be of benefit to all concerned.

A Fair Brexit

One additional element of labour market reform, following withdrawal from the EU, concerns the degree of employment and social protection accorded to those working in the UK labour market. To address concerns raised by trade unionists and other campaigning organisations, the government has made a number of commitments in this area (Conservative Party, 2017:7,12,16,36). However, there remains anxiety over whether these employment protections will be rolled back once the immediate Brexit process is completed.[8] This undermines trust in the Brexit process and creates unnecessary uncertainty for working people and their families.

This is unnecessary. Most employment rights stem from, or are guaranteed by, UK and not EU law – i.e. unfair dismissal, minimum wage, redundancy pay, paternity rights and shared parental leave, flexible working and industrial relations legislation. EU law does have an impact in the area of maternity leave, although UK law already extends beyond the EU minimum and parental leave is unpaid.

Where UK law would have to be extended to provide the same level of protection as current EU directives, most of these should be unproblematic. For example, it is unlikely that UK politicians would wish to roll back protection against discrimination nor go into a General Election promising to reduce the number of paid holidays guaranteed to employees. Given the earlier discussion about the impact of casualization on the UK labour market, protection afforded to agency, part-time and fixed term workers should be equally straightforward to agree.

A Left Brexit approach could, however, go further. To ensure that workers and their families benefit from the reconfigured labour market as well as business interests, it could seek to develop a new social contract between the British people. This could include initiatives to promote employee voice, through collective bargaining together with other forms of participation and engagement at work. It could use the Brexit dividend (from no longer having to contribute directly to the EU budget) to improve public services and public infrastructure, as was suggested by campaigning groups at the time of the referendum.

A new social contract would allay the concerns of those who fear that Brexit might be used as a means to further erode the social and employment protections of working people. Instead, Brexit could prove to be the catalyst for the strengthening and renewing of our social obligations to one another. A Brexit truly for the many and not just the few.

Challenge Five – Rebalancing the UK Economy

The weaknesses in the UK economy, discussed thus far, indicate the presence of structural rather than temporary issues for policy makers to solve. To his credit, former Chancellor of the Exchequer, George Osborne, correctly identified many of these problems.[9] Indeed, some of his proposed solutions around the rejuvenation of the manufacturing sector (the 'march of the makers') and seeking to ensure that growth benefitted all parts of the economy (starting with the Northern Powerhouse project) were along the right lines.[10] Sadly, though, the means of making these changes were insufficiently well thought out and resourced. As a result, only limited progress has been made on most of these objectives.[11]

One element that was always missing from these earlier proposals was the need for a supportive macroeconomic strategy which ensured a sufficient level of demand in the economy to encourage investment and expanded production. Supply side reforms are important but, in isolation, are not sufficient. Moreover, the nature of the industrial strategy required to make a substantial impact upon the UK economy – encouraging the creation of additional manufacturing capacity and pioneering investments in new markets and new technologies – requires a greater magnitude of investment and willingness for government agencies to use the full range of available policy tools to steer markets than has been thus far accepted.

Brexit has, however, changed the calculations. There is a more pressing need to engage with the rebalancing strategy in order to create a more resilient economy; one more suited to take advantage of whatever opportunities that Brexit may reveal. Evidence of this can be seen both in the evolution of the current government's thinking on such issues, and more strikingly in Labour's proposals relating to its industrial strategy and National Transformation Fund. Both propose using the greater independence of action that Brexit can potentially deliver in order to transform the UK economy. There is disagreement on many of the details, of course, but the broad thrust of the necessity for this new economic strategic approach is broadly recognised.

Developing an Active Industrial Policy
An essential element of this more active policy framework concerns the development of an active industrial policy.

After years of neglect, with only passing lip service paid to the notion of government involvement in the creation of a support structure to promote and support the UK industrial base, the need for a more active form of industrial policy of one form or another is now accepted by all of the main political parties. Indeed, the revitalisation of industrial strategy has been accepted as an essential element in rebalancing the UK economy and creating an economy that works for everyone across the UK (Conservative Party, 2017:12-13; Labour Party, 2017:13-15).

It was, for example, explicitly stated, in the Prime Minister's 2017 Lancaster House speech, that the development of a more active form of industrial strategy was designed to ensure that all areas of the UK were better prepared to take advantages of whatever opportunities that Brexit presented.[12] Whilst a significant element of Labour's promise to create 'an economy that works for all' would involve a £250bn 'National Transformation Fund' intended to upgrade the UK economy (Labour Party, 2017:11-15).

Whilst there are significant differences in scale and in the detail about how industrial strategy is to be implemented, there is at least a degree of shared vision that it must go beyond 'horizontal' measures – i.e. creating a good climate for investment and skills development – to embrace more 'vertical' interventions, such as focusing support on industries with the greatest future growth potential and enabling the development of more comprehensive UK-based supply chains (Conservative Party, 2017:19; Labour Party, 2017:14-15).

One element in any industrial strategy relates to infrastructural investment. This assists business development by reducing the costs related to transportation of goods and accessing a wider skilled workforce, in addition to increasing the accessibility and speed of internet connections. Better infrastructure facilitates better and cheaper goods and services.

But it is additionally an important component in a macroeconomic strategy which underpins this whole approach. Businesses will not produce or invest unless they expect to be able to sell their goods or services at a profit. Therefore, it is important to manage aggregate demand to maintain this optimum level. There is plenty of evidence to show that demand impacts upon the rate of investment, which changes the stock of capital and thereby affects productive capacity and employment (Rowthorn, 1995, 1999; Alexiou and Pitelis, 2003:628). Moreover, there is a feedback-loop, whereby a larger capital stock will permit a higher level of aggregate demand, and hence both higher output and employment, without resulting in an increase in inflation.

Public investment in infrastructure has been shown to 'crowd in' private investment, as firms in the private sector pick up these contracts and expand their operations, thereby increasing their ability and desire to employ more workers and invest greater sums in new machinery and new technology (Aschauer, 1990).

The importance of infrastructural spending has not been lost upon the Chancellor of the Exchequer, Philip Hammond (HM Treasury, 2016b). However, there is not yet a firm relationship that has been established at the heart of economic policy that identifies the crucial role of aggregate demand as the driver of the economy. Instead, infrastructural spending is viewed rather in isolation, as a stand-alone economic instrument rather than as an integrated overall economic approach. This needs to change if the UK is to create the high growth macroeconomic framework within which firms wish to expand, entrepreneurs wish to invest and consumers to continue to spend. In short, macroeconomic policy requires a Keynesian foundation to be truly effective (Whyman and Petrescu, 2017:268-9).

A second element in an industrial strategy relates to the promotion of investment in research and development (R&D). Many of the innovations developed by the private sector with which we are very familiar, were founded upon publically funded research or ideas first developed in state funded universities (Mazzucato, 2015). The foundation technologies lying behind many of the innovative consumer electronics developed by Apple can be linked back to publically funded research. And it is a similar story with many of the advances in renewable energy and clean technologies.

The most notable examples of a more active industrial strategy include Japan, South Korea, Taiwan, Singapore and China. But it also includes the USA, given that the state financed between half and two-thirds of national R&D expenditure between the 1950s and 1980s, principally in the fields of defence-aerospace and healthcare, and it is in many of these areas where the US subsequently established a technological lead (Chang, 2009:2-8). Thus, an industrial policy should aim to eliminate the investment gap that currently exists between the UK and many other comparable OECD economies, in terms of spending on R&D and university research.[13]

A third element concerns the shaping and creation of markets. Government has the ability to create a direction for technological change and, by investing according to this vision, new firms and new markets will be created (Mazzucato, 2015:5). The American government funded much of the development underpinning the IT revolution, including the creation of the internet itself, whilst the worldwide-web was developed by a British academic to facilitate information-sharing between scientists in universities and research institutes throughout the world.

There is often market failure in the development of new markets and new industries, since they often use untried technologies or their sales potential is unknown. Therefore, it often requires public funding of one form or another to have the courage and far-sighted vision to establish a presence in what could become a fast growing important market of the future.

The criticism often levied against this type of market creation is that such 'picking winners' can fail. Certainly. But it is exactly the same with private equity markets and venture capitalists. They do not always succeed. The important point is that there are plenty of examples where state investment in emerging or strategic sectors has succeeded – whether car production in Japan or steel in South Korea. In these examples, the state had the long term vision often lacking in financial markets more focused upon short term gains (Chang 2002). Indeed, for Rodrik (2004:25), if governments make no mistakes when operating an active industrial policy, it implies that they are not trying sufficiently hard.

A good starting point, for market creation, is to identify sectors with good productive growth potential. Emergent sectors, such as alternative energy and those developing applications from new materials, are of particular interest since there are fewer established firms dominating these markets. Examples could include battery technology capable of powering the new fleet of electric cars which government wishes to dominate new car sales by 2030. This is a good example of government steering the creation of future demand, but this needs to be followed up with a substantial R&D programme aimed at creating a cheaper and longer lasting battery for these vehicles. Similarly, renewable energy requires more efficient means of storage to enable supply to better match demand. Thus, research into lithium-air, sodium-ion and redox flow batteries, could lead to a new lucrative UK industry whilst simultaneously create a greener and more efficient energy supply for the future.

A second example might be to focus upon applications of new materials such as graphene, which was discovered at the University of Manchester and for which two academics won the 2010 Nobel Prize in Physics. Graphene is the thinnest known material yet discovered, yet is also the strongest; indeed, it is estimated to be 100 times stronger than steel. Despite being crystalline in structure, it is quite elastic and has the best thermal conductivity of any material. As a consequence, the range of potential applications to which this substance can be put signifies the potential gains for those organisations that are able to establish themselves as first-movers in these markets.

Yet, despite graphene being discovered in Manchester, the UK has filed less than 1% of graphene-related patents (IPO, 2015:7). China, by contrast, has 29% of patents, and South Korea 25% (IPO, 2015:7-9). The response by the UK government, has been to establish a £235 million advanced manufacturing research centre at the University of Manchester (HM Treasury, 2014b:50). This is a welcome but rather belated recognition of the significance of this sector. A more active (rather than reactive) industrial policy, by contrast, might have been expected to move more rapidly to secure greater advantage for the UK economy.

A third option would be to identify those types of technologies which have scale or agglomeration economies, and which are unlikely to receive sufficient long term investment in the absence of public intervention. There are a number of reasons why this may be the case. It may be that certain industries are capital intensive and thereby requiring a substantial initial fixed-cost outlay before economies of scale can be realised (e.g. the national grid, telecommunications networks or the railways). Or alternatively it might be that financial markets perceive that investments are too risky or too long term to realise reasonable shorter term profits (e.g. aerospace in the 1970s).

Technologically advanced or innovative industries are also often a problem for private investors, given that innovation is fundamentally uncertain, and hence it is problematic to accurately predict the probability of success. Hence, innovation requires the type of patient, long-term finance that state investment banks or other forms of public investment are perhaps more capable of providing, alongside a supportive policy environment designed to support high-tech and high growth business development. Industrial policy could, therefore, provide assistance for these activities but it would do so less by identifying specific industries to receive public support, but rather the specific types of technological innovation to promote (Rodrik, 2004:14). This is the framework that some have characterised as an 'entrepreneurial state' (Mazzucato and Penna, 2014:23).

Alongside the provision of funding for dynamic industries or areas of technological innovation, industrial policy has the potential to create a supportive business environment within which these firms can operate. Given that innovation can be constrained by the lack of demand for the resulting products or activities, particularly where large initial investments are required to realise the innovative gains, businesses are likely to remain cautious or slow to innovate unless they are confident about future market conditions (Rodrik, 2004:4,12-13).

Expectations about future profitability is the motivation behind future investment, whilst realised past profits largely finance such investment (Keynes, 1936:135-141; Kalecki, 1971). Moreover, historical evidence would suggest that investment tends to be concentrated where capital productivity is growing the fastest (Baumol et al, 1989). Thus, if industrial policy can contribute towards stimulating industrial expansion and enhancing total factor productivity, it should enhance broader economic policy objectives. There are clear synergies between macroeconomic and industrial policy; the former can create a supportive structure within which the latter can better operate, whilst the latter can stimulate industrial expansion and thereby support macroeconomic goals.

The UK's typically short-termist financial system has not proven to be as helpful to the productive sector as in many other countries. Indeed, many of the criticisms made by Hutton (1994) more than two decades ago still seem remarkably relevant today.[14] Hence, renewed interest in reforming the financial system to promote longer term (more patient) investment, would be welcome (Mazzucato, 2015:65). Interesting ideas along these lines have been advanced by the IPPR Commission on Economic Justice (Sterling and King, 2017). Moreover, policy makers have shown renewed interest in replicating the success demonstrated in Germany, South Korea and the USA, of providing necessary funding for emergent industries through a combination of expanding the range of venture capital funds and/or national or regional investment banks. A reformed and augmented British Investment Bank and or a system of regional development banks could play a significant role in this respect.

Industrial policy could further facilitate the industrial restructuring which will inevitably follow Brexit. Depending upon which option is eventually agreed with between the UK and the EU, there may be a useful role for industrial policy to play in the repositioning of European supply chains. It could ease the transition through provision of information, the financing of infrastructure improvement and compensation for externalities (Lin and Monga, 2010). Indeed, Rodrik (2004:15) notes that industrial restructuring rarely occurs in the absence of government involvement and assistance.

Industrial policy could also be used as a means of assisting those sectors, such as vehicle manufacture, which could face increased costs as a result of border delays or the imposition of tariffs. Should this occur, it is worth noting that the car industry undertakes considerable research and development (R&D), and WTO rules allow for state support for this activity to be provided up to three quarters of the total cost. This would appear to be an obvious means of achieving a 'double dividend' in terms of negating additional costs for a strategically important industry whilst simultaneously most likely increasing investment and productivity in the process.

Brexit has proven to be a useful catalyst for the increased interest in a more active form of industrial policy. This is both because it is probably needed to smooth certain aspects of restructuring in the UK economy, but additionally because certain Brexit options could provide additional freedom of manoeuvre for industrial policy measures.

Current EU competition rules are part of the single market and therefore would form part of the EEA. They are also likely to form part of any customs union agreement, if this follows the Turkish model. In order to promote a single European market, these rules seek to prevent state aid or assistance from disproportionately benefitting a firm or a group of firms. This would make it more difficult for UK industrial policy to favour UK producers without the same benefits being available to other producers across the EU.

It is similarly more difficult (though not impossible) to frame procurement rules to assist local businesses even if this is intended to grow local economies and provide environmental benefits. Previous initiatives to promote 'buy British' or 'buy local' campaigns have been ruled to breach EU competition rules. After Brexit, however, there would be greater scope to use procurement to promote key national interests in the development of the high tech UK manufacturing sector – whether this be in purchasing trains for a publically-owned network or ships for the Royal Navy or local food from local farmers for our schools and hospitals.

There are exceptions that the EU does allow in certain circumstances, and these are given in the Treaty on the Functioning of the European Union (TFEU) – in particular, the Competition Article 101 (EU, 2010:88-9), State ownership Article 106 (EU, 2010:90-1) and the State aid Article 107 (EU, 2010:91-2). These are mainly aimed at allowing certain state assistance in low income areas, suffering serious underemployment. Outside of EU membership, the UK need not necessarily be bound by these rules – at least, if it chose FTA or WTO forms of Brexit.

That is not, however, to suggest that an independent UK could do whatever it liked to favour its own industries. There are still international rules, upheld by the WTO, which govern state interventions of this type.[15] However, the important point here is that these tend to be less restrictive than EU rules. For example, one exception concerns measures that promote regional regeneration or the restructuring of certain industrial sectors; particularly responding to changes in trade and economic policies such as presumably the impact of Brexit. Another exception includes the encouragement of research and development, especially in high tech industries, or assisting the development of infant industries. In addition, an exception to WTO rules can be made in the introduction of local preference in public procurement and when avoiding environmental problems (Rubini, 2004:152).

Government action cannot, moreover, be judged as distorting a market where this market has been newly created, since there is no historical precedent against which to assess any distortion arising from public policy actions (Bohanes, 2015:8). That is why industrial policy can be more effective in emerging sectors as there are fewer limitations upon the type of measures that can be employed.

All of these exceptions to the WTO rules would be available to an independent UK, seeking to rebalance its economy through promoting manufacturing industry, and ensuring that economic growth spread more evenly across the whole nation.

Even within the WTO restrictions, there are plenty of scenarios in which industrial policy can be effective. For example, R&D credits targeted at a specific segment of the market may disproportionately advantage firms in the domestic market, but the benefit is not exclusive and therefore would be allowable. Similarly, non-discriminatory product or hygiene standards may provide disproportionate benefit to the domestic industry, perhaps through the application of labelling standards promoting consumer demand for specific products, but this would be within the scope of WTO rules (Bohanes, 2015:13).

3

Making a Choice – What Type of Brexit?

The creation of a resilient economy, capable of taking advantage of the opportunities available to an independent UK, depends upon the resolution of long standing weaknesses and the transformation of the industrial base to create new highly skilled job opportunities. Key to creating this stronger economy is eliminating current long standing weaknesses in productivity growth, capital formation, the balance of trade, the labour market and ultimately aiming to rebalance the economy.

To achieve these goals, economic policy will itself need to be transformed. It will need to pay more regard to the management of demand in the economy if it is to encourage an improvement in capital formation and tackle the uncertainty surrounding the Brexit process. It will need more active intervention in the areas of skills development and the rebuilding of the UK's manufacturing base. This is best achieved through a coordinated combination of active labour market and active industrial policies.

Hence, policy makers must have the ability to utilise their full set of tools in order to get the economy in its best shape to meet the challenges of the future. Indeed, it is an essential prerequisite for a prosperous long term future as an independent nation. Given the significance of delivering on this economic agenda, it would seem to be an obvious step for the UK to select whichever form of future trade relationship with the EU and rest of the world that would best facilitate this economic transformation.

Up until now, the tendency has been to focus on the different options for trading with the EU in the future – choose one and hope the rest simply falls into place. But *this is the wrong way around*. Consideration of the main options around which the UK could negotiate a meaningful and mutually advantageous future relationship with the EU is necessary, but not by itself sufficient, in order to decide what sort of arrangement would best suit as many people across the whole of the UK as possible. That depends upon the type of economy and society we would like to build in the post-Brexit world.

What is needed is for policy makers, therefore, is to *first* consider what kind of UK they would like to see following withdrawal from the EU. *Then* to decide what economic measures they need to take to make sure that they can realise that vision. And *only subsequently* to choose whichever future trading relationship with other countries that supports these other choices.

Choosing the form of Brexit to negotiate with the EU before identifying the challenges that need to be addressed, and the opportunities which should be grasped, is the wrong way of looking at the problem. It is putting the cart before the horse. That is why I have deliberately chosen to focus on the economic challenges facing the UK before turning to consider the main Brexit options available for us to pursue – because these options need to be capable of aiding the transformation of our economy rather than getting in its way.

What are the Main Brexit Options?

The final agreement between the UK and the EU on the type of economic relationship between the two parties will undoubtedly be a bespoke rather than an 'off the peg' arrangement. Nevertheless, it is worthwhile considering the different types of relationships that the EU currently has with other nations in order for us to be able to judge which type of arrangement would best suit the UK economy and society. The four main options are illustrated in Figure 4.

Figure 4: Options for the Future UK Trade Relationship with the EU

WTO (MFN)	FTA	CU	EEA	Full EU membership
Greenland, USA, ROTW	Canada, South Korea, Switzerland (bilateral)	Turkey, Isle of Man	Norway, EFTA *Rule taker*	*Rule maker*

Greater Independence ──────────────────────────► Greater Access

WTO	FTA	CU	EEA
Tariffs are set at MFN level (currently trade-weighted average for G less than 2%, but agriculture 13.9%)	No tariffs (G, some S)	No tariffs (G, some S)	No tariffs (G, most S)
Probably not agriculture/fisheries	Probably not agriculture/fisheries	May not include agriculture/fisheries & procurement	Harmonised regulations
No requirement on regulations, although exporters always have to abide by rules of external market	Equivalent regulations	Equivalent standards	Accept 4 freedoms
No budgetary cost	No requirement to accept 4 freedoms	Accept CET – no rule of origin regulations but no independent trade deals	Budgetary cost (est. half current cost)
No CET – need rule of origin regulations but can make own trade deals	No budgetary cost	No requirement to accept 4 freedoms	No CET – need rule of origin regulations but can make own trade deals
	No CET – need rule of origin regulations but can make own trade deals	Smaller budgetary cost	

(i) EEA (Norway) Option

The first Brexit option is membership of the European Economic Area (EEA). This would involve the UK re-joining the European Free Trade Association (EFTA), and applying for EEA membership in the same way as current EFTA countries Norway, Iceland and Liechtenstein. This is the deepest form of economic relationship with the EU that is currently available to non-member states.

The EEA option is often described by supporters as the UK staying in the EU's single market (Open Britain, 2018:3). This is not strictly true, as the UK would need to apply to re-join EFTA in order to gain access to the EEA. But this is simply a matter of procedure. More importantly, however, the EEA does not include all aspects of the single market. For example, it does not include agricultural goods and there are certain areas where standards and regulations are not harmonised but are rather mutually recognised, which means they do not have to be identical but only similar. This is not a particularly significant issue for goods, but is more significant for certain service exporters. Thus, it is perhaps more accurate to say that the EEA agreement encompasses many (but not all) aspects of the single market to its participants.

The advantages of the EEA are primarily that it provides for tariff free trade in goods and some services, as currently occurs between the UK and the EU. Because it does not include a customs union, participants are free to negotiate trade deals with third parties. It would be possible to graft a customs union agreement on to the EEA if parties agreed. However, this would be rather problematic for any UK government, given that this would be virtually indistinguishable from current full EU membership except that the UK would no longer have a vote in determining the rules that it would have to accept to maintain market access. Hence, this would hardly be a realistic option.

One consequence of the EEA remaining outside of the EU's customs union is that, like all other forms of preferential trade agreement, exporters within EEA countries would have to comply with 'rule of origin' regulations, to prevent third countries tariff hopping. This occurs where signatories of a FTA levy different tariff rates and exporters in a third country try to evade the higher tariffs in one FTA country by exporting to the lower tariff FTA nation and then re-exporting the same goods at zero additional tariff cost. Rule of origin regulations prevent this by specifying a minimum percentage of the value of the good that has to originate in each FTA nation. If a good fails this test, it is treated as originating outside of the FTA and full tariffs are applied.

There have been a number of studies which have sought to quantify how much rule of origin requirements add to the costs of exports. For economies of the North American Free Trade Agreement (NAFTA), this has been estimated to be around 1.8% of export values (Anson et al, 2004; Carrere and De Melo, 2004). For the UK, this direct cost is likely to be lower, given that the price of purchasing a certificate of origin from the Chamber of Commerce is currently only around £30.

There is a further indirect impact if the rule of origin regulations causes exporters to switch to alternative (local) suppliers to qualify under the rule (Lowe, 2018). This might be a concern for certain UK producers. For example, the rule of origin threshold for car exports from South Korea to the EU currently stands at 55% of total value, which might prove problematic to UK car manufacturers whose products only currently rate around 41% domestic content.[1]

One way around this regulation is to negotiate a lower

baseline for domestic content. Another is for UK exporters to source more of their supply chain locally. The latter might incur higher costs for companies – one study estimates that this could push the total cost of rule of origin regulations to around 4.3% (World Bank, 2005:70). But, once again, the equivalent figure for the UK is likely to be lower, given the fact that the EU has already sought to ease this process for other non-member nations through the implementation of a Pan-Euro-Mediterranean (PEM) convention, which will replace the need for bilateral rules of origin protocols with a single simplified approach.[2]

In addition, whilst rule of origin regulations may impose a cost upon individual exporters, there is also potential benefit to the economy as a whole. For example, if parts of the supply chain did indeed switch from international to local suppliers, there would be a resultant gain to the UK economy which would partially or wholly offset any increase in exporter costs. In addition, any potential increase in costs for exporters could, additionally, be partially or fully negated by the use of industrial policy measures, such as the use of targeted R&D tax breaks, support for the development of new supplier clusters and/or the training of a specialised workforce to meet the new needs of an expanded local supply chain. If this were the case, the result may very well be a net benefit for the UK as domestic activity would have been boosted as a result. It would also have an environmental advantage, given the reduction in the transportation of parts between geographically distant parts of a wider supply chain network.

There are, furthermore, certain benefits derived from country of origin marking, including consumers using it as a proxy for the quality of goods and services (Hui and Zhou, 2002). Country of origin labelling would facilitate a 'buy

British' campaign, of the type currently forbidden by EU rules but which would be available to policy-makers post-Brexit. The evidence is that these campaigns, if designed correctly, can have a positive economic impact, both for UK exporters but also for domestic producers reducing import penetration (Chisik, 2003; Dinnie, 2008).

A second disadvantage of EEA membership concerns the fact that EFTA states have to accept the primacy of rules and regulations set by the EU for the single market. They have the right to consultation before decisions are taken, but they do not have the ability to directly determine the rules by which they have to abide. EFTA states do have a theoretical right of veto, in that they can refuse to accept new rules designed by the EU from coming into force in their territory. However, this has never been exercised because it would prevent all EFTA nations from continuing to trade freely in the EU single market. As a result, critics have described EEA members as 'rule-takers' rather than 'rule-makers' – in effect, being little more than a client or vassal state. Indeed, Norway has itself expressed significant concerns over this aspect of the EEA (NOU, 2012a,2012b).

Advocates of the EEA option suggest that the governance of the agreement by the EFTA surveillance Authority, not the European Court of Justice, lessens the impact.[3] Moreover, it is possible that losing the right to vote on the regulations that affect its economy might make less practical difference than might be anticipated. After all, critics of current EU membership have often pointed to the frequency of the UK being out-voted on various issues of national interest. Nevertheless, it is still hard to conclude that the EEA would not relegate the UK to acting as rule-taker rather than rule-maker in certain important areas. Certainly, this has been the conclusion reached by the CBI (2013:16).

The fact that EU competition rules apply to EEA members means that it would be more difficult for the UK to utilise state aid or other industrial strategy mechanisms to grant what the EU would regard as unfair advantages over competitors. The implications of this were discussed in the earlier section on industrial strategy.

The EEA would additionally require the UK to continue to accept the 'four freedoms', which prohibit restrictions upon the movement of capital and labour. This makes effective control of migration from other EU member states impossible to achieve. But, perhaps more profoundly, it prevents more effective national controls over the movement of capital. At a time when the flow of 'hot' money and the excesses of the financial sector have inflicted such damage to the real economy, consideration of a tighter regulatory approach might have been anticipated. However, the imposition of tighter regulations would fall foul of the 'four freedoms' test if it restricted the flow of capital between signatories to the EEA agreement, and would therefore not be permissible in all but emergency situations.

Membership of the EEA would necessitate public procurement remaining open to companies from all EEA signatories. It would require telecommunications and transportation to be liberalised. Moreover, all company mergers in EEA nations are subject to the EU Commission. This has implications for those political parties in the UK who may wish to consider the renationalisation[4] of certain utility companies, or to use public procurement as one tool in a broader industrial strategy aimed at revitalising the national economy. It has also been perceived to be a problem for certain EFTA nations, since they often have higher safety standards than the EU norm, and therefore EEA participation requires them to be simplified or lower technical standards adopted, to ensure common rules apply throughout the single market (USITC, 2000:2-17).

EEA membership would, additionally, be likely to require the UK to make a financial contribution to EU programmes as a quid pro quo for access to its markets. Indeed, despite it not being a relatively small country and not member of the EU, Norway is the tenth largest contributor to EU activities (NOU, 2012a:784). If Norway's payments are any guide, this may equate to between £4.4 and £6 billion per year, depending upon whether the UK rebate continues to operate in this new arrangement (Whyman and Petrescu, 2017:314-5).

Finally, since participation in the Schengen area is currently part of its framework, acceptance of the EEA would represent an extension to the free movement of people than the UK has to date accepted.

(ii) Customs Union (Turkey) Option

The second option for the UK to consider would be to negotiate a new customs union with the EU. This would, in large part, revert the trade relationship between the UK and the EU back to what existed when the UK joined the EU in 1973, until the advent of the single market in 1992. Thus, the adoption of the customs union Brexit option would involve us leaving the EU of today, only to travel back in time to recreate the essence of the organisation we joined in 1973.

The customs union option has precedent since a partial customs union was agreed between Turkey and the EU in 1996. This is only partial because it covers goods but not agricultural products, services or procurement.[5]

Customs unions promote free trade in the same way as a Free Trade Agreement (FTA), but in addition all participants adopt a common external tariff and common commercial policy.

There are a number of advantages to customs unions. The first is that, unlike the EEA, customs unions (and FTAs) are primarily focused upon the creation of free trade in goods. Hence there would be no automatic requirement to accept other add-on aspects of full EU membership, such as the Common Agricultural Policy or the free movement of labour and capital.

A second advantage would be to negate the need to introduce rule of origin regulations and related customs declarations, to prove the provenance of the goods the UK would wish to sell into the EU marketplace. Indeed, customs unions are the only existing form of preferential trade arrangement whereby exporters would not be required to comply with rule of origin regulations.

The head of HM Revenue and Customs (HMRC), Jon Thompson, recently suggested that the cost of this additional bureaucratic burden on UK businesses could be in the region of £17-20bn[6]. This estimate does seem to be rather excessive. Indeed, later analysis of his figures would seem to indicate that this headline figure is based upon a number of quite questionable assumptions. By contrast, Gudgin and Mills calculate the figure to be closer to £3.6bn.[7] This is still a significant figure, although the cost would be offset by the raising of tariff revenues for those categories of goods not included in any form of preferential free trade agreement.

A third potential advantage for customs unions is that there might be an additional short term cost saving in deferring costs associated with the updating the UK's customs and border systems. This investment would be necessary for the introduction of a smart borders approach that is likely to form part of any other trade regime with the EU. The introduction of new scanners, surveillance technology at borders and accompanying software would be expensive.

This is only likely to be a temporary cost saving, however, as smart border technology would facilitate smoother trade and passenger travel across borders for all UK markets, not just those of the EU. Hence, many of these innovations are likely to be introduced at some stage in any case. The fact that the UK currently replies upon unsatisfactory data which cannot specify, with accuracy, the numbers of people entering and leaving its borders at any given time, will hamper efforts to design a rational manpower policy aimed at meeting the needs of domestic industry. Moreover, a more sophisticated monitoring of goods transit would help to target criminal activity. Thus, whilst the establishment of a new customs union relationship with the EU might defer some of these technologies being introduced, it is unlikely to do so permanently.

A final advantage of customs unions is that they have also been advanced as the only realistic way of avoiding some sort of border check on goods flowing across borders. This is one reason why this option is being promoted by the EU negotiators as a solution to the issue of avoiding re-imposing border controls between the Republic of Ireland and Northern Ireland. It is not, however, strictly accurate to present customs unions in this way – other potential solutions exist, such as 'smart' border or customs partnership proposals. Both are discussed a little later in this section.

It should be noted, however, that whilst customs unions might negate the need for border checks for goods passing between participating nations, it does nothing to deal with the movement of *people*. Consequently, if the UK wish to deviate from the EU policy of the free movement of labour, then the determination to comply with the Good Friday agreement would require the adoption of smarter (max-fac) technology to facilitate flows of people across the Irish border.

There are, however, a number of downsides to customs unions. The first relates back to what they are supposed to achieve, namely to increase trade and reduce costs by removing tariffs between participants. In economics terminology, dating back to Viner (1950), this is called trade creation and is generally considered to be a net economic benefit. However, it does so by building a tariff wall around the combined economy of the participants, and in so doing prevents countries from importing other goods from elsewhere in the world as cheaply as before, because of the extra tariff tax levied on these imports.

Customs unions can also lead to importers switching from formerly more efficient and cheaper producers, outside the tariff wall, towards less efficient but now cheaper (after tariffs are taking into consideration) producers within the customs union. This might bring additional economic activity within the participants combined economies, but it does so at an increased cost for consumers. This is known as trade diversion and generally considered to be a net economic loss. Indeed, there is a fair amount of evidence to suggest that this is precisely the economic effect that occurred in the early years of the UK joining the EU (Miller and Spencer, 1977:82-90; Portes, 2013:F5-6).

Hence, the net economic effect of the formation of customs unions is by no means certain. Since the UK is currently in a customs union with the EU, transferring to a new version of customs union will not necessarily result in any observable net further loss or gain, but it would preclude potential gains that could be generated by choosing alternative trade relationships.

A second downside is that participants cannot negotiate their own trade arrangements with third countries. Instead, this is the sole jurisdiction of the customs union as a whole. Moreover, a single member cannot vary its tariff rates from the common tariff. Thus, should the UK wish to forge closer trading ties with former Commonwealth countries, as existed before the UK joined the EU, it could not do so by negotiating its own trade deals nor setting preferential tariffs with these nations if it were part of a customs union arrangement with the EU. The same if it wanted to negotiate a trade deal with the USA or China. Similarly, if the UK wanted to take advantage of its independence by lowering tariff barriers on the import of food at world prices, to take advantage of cheaper prices whilst additionally aiding economic growth in developing nations, it would be prevented from doing so within a customs union.

One asymmetric feature of a customs union agreement is that the EU would not be prevented from undertaking its own future trade negotiations with other countries and the UK would be expected to abide by the decisions taken by the EU in these matters. This is likely to result in the UK having to allow other nations, with whom the EU has agreed a trade agreement, free access to UK markets *but without the assurance that the UK would have similar free access to their markets*, unless the UK subsequently negotiated a separate voluntary agreement with this other nation. There is no reason to necessarily presume that this would necessarily be forthcoming, since this nation would have already gained the benefit of full UK market access without having to concede reciprocal rights to UK exporters. Indeed, Turkey has fallen foul of this particular problem with its customs union with the EU, as South Africa and Algeria refused to conclude a reciprocal trade agreement with Turkey, meaning that they had the benefit of enjoying preferential access to Turkish markets whilst Turkish exporters did not enjoy similar terms.[8] This is an aspect of customs unions that particularly exercised the CBI (2013:148-9).

Thirdly, since both EEA and Swiss bilateral agreement options require EFTA nations to make a net financial contribution to EU activities, it is almost certain that this would be expected by the UK. This is not an issue for Turkey, because it is a net recipient of EU development support.

Fourthly, whilst customs unions may eliminate tariff barriers, they may not prevent administrative or regulatory non-tariff barriers, which may impose a cost upon exporters. This is likely to be a factor for all forms of trade where common standards are not imposed by the EU.

Fifthly, if the customs union agreement between the EU and Turkey provides the model for any similar arrangement with the UK, then this agreement would require the UK to comply with EU commercial and competition policy, together with the acquis communautaire. Thus, Turkey has to comply with a similar range of EU-determined rules and regulations as would apply as a member of the EEA. In addition, to settle any possible disputes that may arise, the European Commission and European Court act as 'impartial' arbiters of the agreement (CBI, 2013:149). This imposes restrictions upon national policy actions in a variety of areas, such as procurement, state aid and the setting of standards and regulatory framework that differs from that of the EU.

In Turkey's case, this 'deep' customs union agreement is intended to facilitate possible future full membership. Hence, Turkey is more concerned with gaining full membership in order to gain a voice in the determination of EU trade policy and the setting of goods standards.[9] The UK's position would be substantially different, given that the UK has voted to withdraw from EU membership and hence will naturally have more interest in varying rules and regulations over which it will have thereby regained control. This may enable the UK to press for a looser adherence to the EU commercial and regulatory framework and yet still benefit from the essential elements of a customs union. However, this is by no means certain. Yet, failure to do so would result in UK policy makers being stymied in their stated intention to develop a substantive and active form of industrial policy, aimed at rebuilding UK manufacturing industry and thereby rebalancing the economy.

The disadvantages of customs unions have led the CBI (2013:12, 148) to conclude that the 'Turkey model' would be 'the worst of the "half-way" alternatives to full EU membership, leaving the UK with very limited EU market access and zero influence over trade deals.' This rejection of the option is a little odd, given that the CBI was a strong advocate of UK entry into the then 'Common Market' in 1975, which was, of course, a customs union. Yet, it is still instructive that, when considering the best alternative model for the UK to pursue in its future trade relationship with the EU after Brexit, the CBI considers customs unions to be inferior to all other options.

Overall, therefore, choosing to establish a new customs union with the EU might be a difficult proposition to 'sell' to a UK electorate which expressed its collective desire to regain greater control over its economic life.

(iii) Smart Borders (Max-Fac)

As mentioned earlier, the use of new technology-driven solutions to ensure maximum facilitation (often termed 'max-fac') of trade flows across borders has been considered by both the UK government and the European parliament as potential solutions to avoid a hard border between

Northern Ireland and the Republic of Ireland (Karlsson, 2017; HMG, 2017). As detailed in the report prepared for the European Parliament, elements of this approach have been used between the USA and Canada, Sweden and Norway, together with Australia and New Zealand (Karlsson, 2017).

The smart borders solution depends upon the creation of a trust-based system, where control is exerted through technology and mobile enforcement away from the immediate border zone; perhaps within a 10 mile radius either side. For individuals, this might involve the use of a registered traveller programme (including pre-departure registration and clearance), biometric passports incorporating RFID chips, automatic car number plate recognition cameras and smart gate scanning facilities. For goods, it might include the mutual recognition of authorised economic operators and individual travellers, electronic pre-arrival clearance approval, duties collected periodically and controlled through audit. There would additionally be technological surveillance of the border thereby allowing physical checks based upon risk assessment and that take place away from the border (perhaps within a 10 mile zone or alternatively at the importers place of business) using mobile control and inspection units.[10]

Many of these solutions are already available for implementation. However, the low cost of the current approach, and the comparatively lighter touch of the current physical inspection regime, has meant that there has not been any great enthusiasm for the introduction of a smarter approach until now.[11]

The key to this approach is the establishment of sufficient trust between the state agencies and the private sector to enable these technical solutions to operate without physical checks slowing the process. This depends upon the sophistication of risk management processes to identify areas of greater concern and focus monitoring in these areas. The more detailed information, provided by smarter border observation should make this easier.

Indeed, given the very poor standard of data currently available to the UK government on the number of people entering and leaving the UK, this element of smarter borders is probably worth investing in in any case. It would assist with any new migration policy, and should help to identify and combat crime more effectively than current approaches. Karlsson (2017:13) argues that this could be seen as an asset the UK brings to the negotiating table in its discussions with the EU and other nations. It is therefore probably a good investment irrespective of whether the UK adopts the 'max fec' model as its preferred approach to ease trade and individual border crossings.

(iv) Customs Partnership

The customs partnership proposals, developed by the UK government, differs from a standard customs union in that the UK would collect tariffs on behalf of EU member states on goods imported into the UK but destined for countries within the EU customs union. However, because the UK would not formally be within a customs union, it would be free to set its own tariffs with the rest of the world, for goods intended solely for the UK market. If UK tariffs were lower than those set by the EU, then UK businesses could claim back the difference from the UK government for those goods they imported and designated for the UK market.

Essentially, there would be a sort of *de facto* customs union in operation between the UK and the EU, in that there would be no need for customs processes for goods flowing between the two, but all other features of a customs union would be absent. This approach would not, for example, include the requirement to abide by a common external tariff (most likely set by the EU). Similarly, the UK would be free to negotiate its own trade deals with the rest of the world. Hence, the customs partnership might be conceived of as lying somewhere between a standard customs union and a FTA 'with benefits'.

It is obvious why the Prime Minister is so interested in this proposal, as it negates some of the most obvious weaknesses with standard customs unions and yet maintains relatively frictionless trade. It could also provide a solution for the issue of border controls (for goods at least) between the Republic and Northern Ireland. Nevertheless, the proposal is untested. It would rely upon technology to track goods and determine the recipients of tariff payments. Hence, it would require similar investment and technological infrastructure as the smart borders approach, but with an added layer of tracking the origin of goods components and accordingly assigning the correct level of tariffs. Without monitoring and robust enforcement, it would be relatively easy to tariff jump – i.e. evading the higher tariff wall by exporting into a cheaper tariff country and from there into the rest of the customs union. Failure to deal with this issue would inevitably lead to the disintegration of the partnership and its evolution into either a standard customs union or a FTA.

Another concern raised by the customs partnership is that it is unlikely to work without very similar or even identical standards and regulations being applied between the UK and the EU. This is an issue recognised in the 2018 UK white Paper, discussed below.

Yet, acceptance of harmonisation would cause a problem for those seeking to use the new independence secured by Brexit to adopt different forms of regulation which would better suit UK circumstances. If this encompassed EU competition regulations, then the customs partnership approach would be no improvement on the Turkish customs union or EEA alternatives in so far as it would inhibit industrial policy measures aimed at rebuilding the UK manufacturing base.

Given that it is complex and untried, it is not surprising that the proposal has received considerable criticism. The Financial Times, for example, regards the system as 'unworkable' and yet, simultaneously, perhaps the governments' best tactical means of winning a vote in the House of Commons on a Brexit plan.[12] If this charge is accurate, then this is obviously a completely unsatisfactory state of affairs – proposing something that will probably not work, in order to win a vote, and then to re-negotiate either a FTA or a customs union option without the same degree of parliamentary scrutiny. However, even if the FT's charge of cynicism is misplaced, it would appear unlikely that the customs partnership approach would prove to be sufficiently rigorous to be mutually accepted by all parties as the core of a future trade arrangement.

(v) UK Government White Paper, 2018

The 2018 White Paper outlines the government's preferred model for the future economic relationship between the UK and the EU (HMG, 2018). This document maintains the line that the UK will be leaving both the single market and the customs union, and will replace current trade cooperation with what it describes as a Free Trade Agreement (FTA). However, in reality, what is proposed is quite different from what is usually contained within a FTA. Indeed, it is actually more of a hybrid of the EEA, customs union and customs partnership approaches.

The rationale behind the proposal is that it is trying to square a very difficult circle. It seeks to ensure as little friction involved in the trade in certain sectors of the economy (i.e. goods and agri-food), which are the hallmarks of the EEA or a customs union, but whilst still retaining control over immigration and regaining the ability to make trade deals with the rest of the world, both of which would not be possible in EEA or customs union approaches.

Its chosen method is to rely upon a combination of four things:

i.   a 'Facilitated Customs Arrangement' (FCA)

ii. smart border technology

iii. acceptance of 'a common rulebook' for goods and agri-food sectors

iv. establishment of a joint committee to monitor and enforce the trade agreement

The FCA combines elements from earlier customs partnership and smart border technology proposals. It is an attempt to forge a new customs union arrangement with the EU but without the customary restrictions upon the UK having to accept the common external tariff and the EU having the sole authority to negotiate trade deals. Instead, the proposal is for the UK to apply the EU's trade policy and collect its tariffs for goods entering UK territory but bound ultimately for the EU marketplace. However, the UK would retain the right to set its own tariffs and trade policy for goods which would be consumed in the UK (HMG, 2018:16). To avoid tariff jumping, the proposal is to charge the higher tariff on all goods unless the eventual destination can be robustly demonstrated in advance, through a trusted trader scheme, and any over-charging could subsequently be reclaimed by importers.

If this was accepted by the EU, it would avoid the need for a rule of origin requirement on all goods exported from the UK to the EU marketplace. However, it does require sophisticated audit trails to ensure the rigorous enforcement of two divergent trade regimes and there are question marks over whether these systems will be in place by the point the UK completes its transition phase post-Brexit, and also whether the EU will accept the principle of what it previously termed 'magical thinking'.[13]

The second element concerns the introduction of smart border technology. As previously discussed, this is intended to act as an alternative to border inspections, if the combination of remote surveillance, intelligence-led customs enforcement and audit trail monitoring can convince all parties of its reliability and ability to prevent the smuggling of goods, people and/or terrorist materials. This is seen as a means whereby there need be no hard borders erected between Northern Ireland and the Republic of Ireland. Once again, however, whilst the objective of establishing smarter border technology over a period of time is likely to form a feature of future border inspection regimes for trade between the UK and all other nations, it is presumptuous, at this early stage in the development of the processes involved, to expect it to demonstrate the rigour required for acceptance by all parties as a means of completely eliminating the need for all border checks in their entirety.

Whilst the first two elements of the White Paper proposals are imaginative, if a little premature given the inadequate preparations being made to develop and roll out the technology, processes and training to users required for successful implementation, the other two elements of the plan are particularly problematic.

The main problem in attempting to enjoy the benefits of a customs union or the EU's single market, without having to be bound by all of the rules (i.e. common external tariff, no independent trade deals and/or acceptance of the freedom of movement of capital, people, goods and services), is that it requires acceptance of either identical or similar rules, regulations and standards. All exporters, when selling into a market, have to meet the rules and standards set by that market. This applies to various aspects of trade, including food safety and hygiene, the safety of toys and/or the application of a minimum level of health and safety standards being applied in the production process (i.e. no slave labour, no sweat shops, etc). The EU currently operates a common system of rules and regulations to cover all of these aspects, and all firms who operate across the EU are expected to abide by these rules. This is irrespective of whether they are exporting to another member state or simply producing for their own domestic market. Since around 94% of all UK firms do not export directly to other EU member states, this is often viewed as an unnecessary regulatory burden.

Most FTAs contain a requirement that each participating nation establishes *equivalence* rather than *harmonised* rules and regulations. The drafters of the White Paper are fully aware of this fact and, indeed, they cite examples whereby similar but not identical rules were agreed as the basis for trade between the EU and countries such as Canada, Chile, Israel, Japan, Korea, Tunisia, the USA and New Zealand (HMG, 2018:23). Hence, if other FTAs do not require harmonisation of standards and other regulations in the area of food, which is likely to be one of the most critical in terms of its potential impact upon human health and wellbeing, then it is not necessary for the successful agreement of a FTA that this occurs.

Yet, despite this precedence, the UK government proposals concede acceptance of 'a common rulebook' for goods and agri-food safety standards. The reason for doing so would appear to be in the attempt to solve one of the problems with the aforementioned customs partnership idea. In the absence of harmonised rules and standards, it would be unlikely that the EU would accept frictionless trade without imposing either a rule of origin requirement or border checks to ensure the compliance of any goods it imports into the single market fully comply with its requirements. This would add to the costs of UK exporters but would also infer the creation of a hard border between Northern Ireland and the Republic of Ireland. The harmonisation of UK with EU standards would be one way around both of these problems.

It is, however, more than a little surprising for a government that insists that it is taking back control for the British people.

Moreover, not only does the White Paper concede that the UK would not deviate from *current* EU rules and regulations pertaining to goods and agri-food, but it proposes to passively accept all *future* rules and regulations introduced by the EU with relevance to these categories of products. And it proposes doing so by international treaty, thereby tying the hands of future governments who might wish to vary some of these regulations if they prove to be onerous for UK producers or consumers.

In accepting complete harmonisation ('a common rule book') for regulations on goods and agricultural produce, the White Paper proposal is closer to EEA and customs union approaches, in that the UK would become a *rule-taker* and have to apply whatever rules or regulations the EU develops for the single market both now and in the future. Even if the UK is allowed to input into the decision-making process leading to the formation of new trade rules, as is currently the case for other EEA nations, there is no reason to believe that this would prove effective in preventing new regulations from being introduced that impose additional burdens on UK producers. Moreover, suggestions that Parliament would have oversight of these rules is largely toothless, as the Norwegian government has found, as any deviation would immediately threaten continued access into the EU single market on preferential terms.

Perhaps the most troubling aspect of this harmonisation of UK with EU rules is in the area of state aid and maintaining significant aspects of current competition regulation (HMG, 2018:38). This makes it much more difficult for the UK to deviate from the EU's current approach to industrial policy. In so doing, it provides a severe constraint upon the ability of any UK government to attempt to rebuild UK manufacturing industry, and through that means to tackle the long standing weaknesses in the economy. It deliberately sets out to bind the hands of successor governments who might wish to use state aid as an element of a more active form of economic policy.

It is interesting to contrast this stance with the declaration made regarding public procurement. Here, the White Paper does not propose maintaining current EU rules and nor should it. A wiser use of procurement policy could provide useful assistance to a more active industrial strategy. Therefore, deviating from current EU restrictions on its use is an intelligent step. But it therefore defies logic as to why the White Paper does not take a similar enlightened position on state aid and competition policy. If one element of this package can be used to rejuvenate the UK economy, why refuse to use all other available economic policy tools? It does not make sense.

The final element of the White Paper plan concerns the establishment of a joint committee to monitor and enforce the trade agreement. At one level, this is not controversial, since all trade agreements require an institutional arrangement of some sort to resolve differences of interpretation. Precedents include FTAs between the EU with both Canada and the Ukraine, whilst the North American Free Trade Agreement (NAFTA) and the Association of Southwest Asian Nations (ASEAN) FTA established a similar institutional framework (HMG, 2018:85).

Yet, at a deeper level, what is proposed in the White Paper is a more troubling proposition for two reasons. Firstly, the White Paper makes the claim that UK courts would no longer be subservient to the Court of Justice of the European Union (CJEU) and that this guarantees UK sovereignty. Yet, it goes on to say that UK courts would need to pay 'due regard' to the decisions made by CJEU (HMG, 2018:84,91-2). Superficially, this statement appears to be little more than acknowledging that national courts often take account of the decisions made by international courts and national courts in other jurisdictions. But given the fact that the White Paper has already conceded that the EU would set the rules and regulations for trade in goods and agri-food, and the EU would wish the CJEU to play the dominant role in the supervision of the trade relationship, it is likely that this concession enables the latter to hold the whip hand in interpreting UK-EU trade rules.[14] Indeed, one of the factors prompting the resignation of the former Brexit Secretary, David Davis, was what he described as 'illusory' claims of Parliamentary control and the fact that harmonisation with EU rules and regulations was not, in any real sense, the UK taking back control over its laws.

Beyond the five main elements of the government's

proposals, there is one more that will be of particular interest to trade unionists and those on the Left. The White Paper commits the UK to maintaining existing workers' rights 'on the day of withdrawal' and further proposes that the UK commits to the 'non-regression of labour standards' (HMG, 2018:40). This is not quite the same as a commitment that the existing range of labour standards and protections will remain unchanged beyond the completion of the withdrawal process, but only that labour standards as a whole should not be markedly reduced. There would appear to be a significant amount of 'wiggle room' inherent in this statement, and it would be an area where clarification should be sought, by trade unions and those on the progressive side of politics, if the White Paper does indeed form the basis for the governments vision for Brexit.

Overall, the White Paper contains a number of interesting ideas, but overall the approach is fraught with difficulties. In attempting to straddle between different Brexit options (i.e. a FTA, customs union and the EEA), it resembles more a bureaucratic box-ticking exercise rather than a consistent plan. It relies upon a number of assumptions and largely untested technologies which, when properly developed, probably do have a role to play in future border arrangements. At present, however, they are insufficiently developed to generate the necessary level of confidence on which to base a complex trade relationship. It is therefore unlikely that the EU negotiators will accept this plan as it is currently constituted without requiring more significant concessions.

The question, therefore, is how this compromise solution evolves. If David Davis is correct[15], and it encourages further compromise, the government may eventually end up accepting either the EEA or customs union options. Both would have some short term advantages in terms of maintaining existing trade flows, but both would impose unnecessary constraints upon the ability of the UK to transform its economy and make the most out of its independent status.

(vi) Free Trade Agreement (Canada) Option

This was the option initially preferred by the Prime Minister[16] and would be the most straightforward approach to establishing a new trade relationship with the EU. This is the most popular form of organised preferential trade agreement across the globe[17] and a number of countries have negotiated a FTA with the EU. These include South Africa, Mexico, South Korea and Canada. Given the enthusiasm with which the EU has begun embarking upon negotiating FTAs with individual countries and groups of nations, it would be slightly surprising if the EU were not interested in doing the same with the UK – i.e. a former member state, with similar (currently identical) standards and a large market for EU goods and services (Springford and Tilford, 2014:9).

A FTA would typically start from the point of the agreement of no tariffs being levied on goods between the partners to the agreement. The inclusion of agri-food is optional. Given the significance the EU places upon the common agricultural policy, it is unlikely that free trade in all foodstuffs will be a realistic goal, without acceptance of common standards. This may be feasible in a number of cases. However, there are others where the UK would be better served by developing its own food standards and, if tariffs were imposed by the EU, to target trade elsewhere in the world.

Under a FTA, the UK would be under no obligation to follow the EU's common tariff regime and it would therefore be free to negotiate its own trade agreements with other countries in the rest of the world. This should result in additional market opportunities and future trade gains. The downside of this is (as with the EEA) is the requirement for rule of origin regulations to establish the provenance of the goods exported to the EU single market. This would impose a (relatively modest) cost on UK exporters and may require some relocation of parts of the supply chain which, as previously discussed may incur certain costs for those firms involved but actually bring additional benefits to the UK economy.

A FTA would require no fiscal contribution to the EU budget, as would be the case for EEA and customs union options. Nor would it involve a commitment to harmonise rules and standards for goods – for most FTA treaties, agreement to mutual recognition of equivalent (but not identical) rules and standards is sufficient. This would enable the replacement of EU with nationally-determined regulations. The evidence is that this might deliver a degree of cost savings for UK firms (Whyman and Petrescu, 2017:176-180).

There would be no requirement for the acceptance of the free movement of labour and capital flows, as would be the case under the EEA. Similarly, there would be no requirement to comply with the single market competition rules – meaning that the use of a more active form of industrial and procurement policy would be both more straightforward to develop and more effective when introduced. A FTA is, therefore, compatible with the more active form of government proposed in this publication.

Like all other options, however, FTAs have their potential downsides. The first relates to concerns over the avoidance of the reintroduction of a hard border between Northern Ireland and the Republic of Ireland. The contortions made by the UK White Paper are partly designed to solve this conundrum. However, they do so through committing to harmonise UK rules and regulations with those of the EU in perpetuity. This unnecessarily constrains the UK's ability to manage its own economy in a different way following the completion of Brexit. It is, therefore, incompatible with the type of FTA proposed in this publication.

The solution to the border issue, which is fully compatible with the type of FTA proposed here, depends upon the introduction of the smarter border approach that has been previously outlined. This will require significant investment in the roll out of the technology and accompanying monitoring software necessary to ensure the success of the approach. It will also require a certain level of trust and goodwill on both sides of the EU-UK border. This may be facilitated by adopting the approach, suggested by former Irish Taoiseach (Prime Minister) Bertie Ahern, that authorities agree to 'turn a blind eye' to any low-scale breaches of any such arrangements, as they are likely to be of little consequence given the size of UK and EU economies respectively.[18] This flexibility might be sufficient for glitches in the rollout of the technology to be resolved.

A second issue which may concern negotiators relates to any suggestion to include third party Most Favoured Nation (MFN) provisions in any FTA agreement. This would automatically extend any benefits arising from any future FTA negotiated by one of the parties (i.e. EU or UK) to the other automatically (CEPR, 2013b:37). These provisions are a two-edged sword, because they would allow the UK to ensure that it benefits from any more favourable trade agreements that the EU is able to negotiate with other nations. But at the same time, they would allow the EU to ensure that the UK could not secure for itself a more favourable trade deal with a third party without the EU having access to the same favourable trade conditions. If one motivation for choosing the FTA option is for the UK to use its ability to negotiate separate trade deals with other nations in order to gain an advantage over its EU competitors, then this would be negated by any third party provisions (CEPR, 2013b:47).

A third negotiating issue would concern the extent to which the EU sought to include 'deeper' elements within the FTA. Examples of this might include the imposition of EU rules on public procurement or competition policy, the oversight of mergers and acquisitions, health and safety rules, labour market regulation, product standards and technical specifications for goods and services entering its market and so forth. Even a compromise for mutual oversight in some or all of these areas would severely reduce the policy freedom of action arising out of Brexit for an independent UK. It would, for example, restrict the range of measures pertaining to employment, company law and could restrain certain measures that could otherwise be taken to rejuvenate UK industrial policy post-withdrawal. Issues pertaining to technical specifications are less problematic because, although sections of UK industry may bemoan the loss of influence upon the development of EU standards, it is nevertheless, the norm for exporters to have to comply with minimum standards set by the countries into which they wish to sell their produce. On balance, it would be better to preserve the policy freedom to be gained by the UK through its independent status, rather than surrender these through accepting these elements to be reintroduced through a deeper form of FTA.

The FTA agreed between the EU and Canada (CETA) is often held up as a good starting point for such negotiations

(Emmerson et al, 2016:15-16). This FTA agreement covers not only goods but also some agricultural products and a significant proportion of services, without the need for Canada to have to make a contribution to the EU budget. Given the significance of the UK's competitive advantage in services, the precedent that CETA demonstrates in what is possible to be included in a FTA with the EU is important.

The former Brexit Secretary, David Davis, advocated a 'Canada plus plus plus' deal, encompassing both goods and services (including financial services). The fact that it received public support from the Italian Economic Development Minister, would suggest that an agreement along these lines might be achievable, despite dismissive statements to the contrary by the EU's chief negotiator, Barnier.[19]

The CETA approach would, however, need to be revised for two main reasons. The first is that the agreement contains what it terms investor protections, whereby a set of substantive rights for foreign investors are established and which set boundaries for national governments to regulate their own economies.[20] This investor-state dispute settlement (SDS) procedure is supposed to protect investor rights against adverse effects stemming from policy decisions enacted by public authorities. The anxiety is that this would provide large trans-national companies with the opportunity to use this process to intimidate national governments by threatening lawsuits if government intervention infringes upon corporate activity.[21] A particular concern has been expressed that investor protection expropriation and equitable treatment standards might cause problems for the delivery and ownership of public services; particularly if national governments wished to re-nationalise areas of public provision (such as the railways) or tighten regulation on public utilities (such as energy and water companies).[22]

Whilst foreign investors do require a degree of protection to safeguard their investments and prevent arbitrary decisions adversely affecting their interests, this has to be balanced against the rights of domestic citizens and the ability of their elected governments to manage their own economies. Tipping this arrangement too far in the interests of large corporations runs the risk of undermining public support for extensions of more basic forms of FTAs. It would run counter to the goal of Brexit, which is for the UK to be able to 'take back control' over its social and economic life.

A second aspect of CETA that has been criticised, particularly by trade unions, concerns the weak proposals related to enforcing those labour rights that the treaty contains.[23] A progressive form of Brexit would aim to secure a broad balance of interests between benefits secured for citizens, workers, public bodies and businesses. Consequently, either the enforcement of labour standards would need strengthening in a future FTA between the UK and the EU, or else the investor protections elements may need stripping back to essentials.

As a result, a decent starting point for FTA discussions between the EU and the UK might be around a shallower form of FTA, which focuses upon trade in goods and a range of services (including finance and business services), and does not extend into deeper areas of trade integration. This would be quicker and simpler to negotiate.

Once in place, it would be possible to consider the rationale for extending this in a number of different areas to create a more progressive form of CETA-plus. This might include a limited number of investor rights, but subject to the democratic superiority of elected government decisions. It might additionally extend the labour rights included in the CETA treaty and provide a more effective means of monitoring their compliance and enforcing these rules where they were not being met. By creating a better balance of interests between corporate interests and citizen rights, this type of more progressive deep FTA might be more attractive to many within the EU, as well as the UK, who would welcome a more enlightened model of trade agreement.

(vii) World Trade Organisation (WTO) Option

The final variant of Brexit relates to the 'no deal' option. This refers to the scenario where it has proven to be impossible to negotiate a mutually satisfactory agreement between the UK and the EU according to the timetable laid out in Article 50 of the Treaty on European Union. The 'no deal' scenario has been described as a 'cliff edge' by many commentators, by which they seek to convey the idea that the failure to reach any sort of agreement with the EU would be a disaster for the UK economy and represent a sudden shock to exporters.

It is certainly true that there are more preferable solutions available to both UK and EU negotiators. But it is questionable whether the 'no deal' option would be quite as damaging as is often suggested (Whyman, 2018).

The failure to reach a trade agreement with the EU would involve all trade between the two parties reverting to being governed by the World Trade Organisation (WTO) trade rules. These prevent trade discrimination, such that the access provided by one country (or group of countries) to another 'most favoured nation' (MFN), has to be available to all other WTO members. In practice, this means that tariffs imposed on UK goods cannot be any higher than those imposed by the EU on their most favoured other trading nations. The exception to this is if a country has negotiated a preferential trade agreement, such as a customs union or

FTA. Accordingly, should the UK revert to trading with the EU according to the WTO scenario, then the level of tariffs likely to be faced by UK exporters are reasonably well known in advance. These range from high levels averaging around 22.3% for agricultural goods to around 2% for non-agricultural goods.[24]

Given that a significant minority of goods are traded tariff-free, the trade-weighted tariff facing UK exporters is likely to only add between 2-3% to their cost base *on average*, which is a sum easily absorbed by UK exporters as it lies within the monthly fluctuations of a floating currency. However, this is only an average. The tariff cost would fall disproportionately upon certain industries, such as car production, chemicals, tobacco, clothing, together with food and beverages. Even here, however, likely tariffs would be only in the range of between 4 and 8%. These costs could easily be offset by industrial policy measures, for example boosting R&D spending or enhancing skills training in these industries. Early formulation of this type of industrial policy assistance would prove helpful in mitigating uncertainty faced by producers in these sectors and unlock otherwise deferred investment decisions.

Exports of services are not subject to tariffs. However they can be disadvantaged by non-tariff barriers (NTBs), which can also affect exports of goods where standards and regulations are not closely aligned between nations. Examples of these could be health and technical barriers on the one hand, which impose legal restrictions upon certain characteristics of goods or services, to administrative regulations which impose a delay or other costs upon trade, thereby reducing the volume traded. NTBs are likely to impose a higher cost upon exporters than formal tariff forms of protectionism, albeit that, like tariffs, NTBs have been declining in significance across the globe over the past few decades. It is therefore probable that the combined effect of tariff and NTBs is likely to have a much smaller impact upon the competitiveness of UK exporters than the boost provided by the post-referendum devaluation of sterling.

It is the case that, in all circumstances other than full participation in the single market (through joining the EEA), UK exporters are likely to experience some degree of NTBs in their dealings with the EU. These are likely to be less intrusive if the UK negotiates a customs union agreement or FTA with the EU. But because regulations and standards would not need to be identical but only equivalent under other forms of trading scheme, there would be scope for bureaucratic delays to occur. Hence, whilst the WTO option may experience more NTBs than under other preferential trade arrangements with the EU, it would be unlikely that it would be the only scenario where these would occur.

To place international trade into context, all World Trade Organisation (WTO) members now have some sort of Preferential Trade Agreement (PTA)[25] with at least one other country or group of countries. It is often suggested that around half of all world trade currently occurs between nations who share a PTA. In reality, this over-estimates their impact, because a sizeable share of this recorded trade is in goods where zero tariffs were already in place before the PTA came into force and hence it had no effect on this element of trade. Accounting for this effect, the WTO estimates that only around 28% of trade occurs on a preferential basis. This is still a significant proportion of world trade, and indeed the figure has probably risen slightly in the few years since the WTO made this calculation. Nevertheless, the WTO estimate suggests that a majority of world trade still occurs using either tariff free or, if tariffs are levied, it takes place according to WTO Most Favoured Nation (MFN) rules (WTO, 2011:7,65).

Trading according to WTO rules doesn't only incur costs. It also offers a number of advantages in relation to other potential trade options. Trading under WTO rules would mean that the UK would not have to abide by current EU rules on the free movement of labour and capital, as would be the case as a member of the EEA. Nor would the UK be required to abide by single market rules and regulations, as would be the case under the EEA and potentially also a customs union if it followed the Turkish model. Being constrained by these rules would make certain policy actions (particularly in relation to industrial policy) more difficult to deliver. We would be free to negotiate whatever trade agreements it wanted with the rest of the world and would have no constraints placed upon it in relation to what tariffs it chose to set on the import of goods from other countries. The UK would pay no contributions to the EU, unless it wished to participate in individual joint programmes (i.e. Erasmus student exchange programmes).

There is one final point that is worth making. Whilst it might generally be expected that there would be a net trade-creating effect extending to all members of one of the different variants of preferential trade agreement, the evidence is not at all clear on whether this actually occurs. The World Bank, for example, has not found unambiguous evidence that this is the case (World Bank, 2005:62).

Considering all of these points, the case against the 'no deal' WTO option is not as overwhelming as many commentators would like us to believe. It is certainly true that the failure to agree a satisfactory preferential trade agreement will incur tariff and some additional non-tariff costs. But these are relatively low in most cases and can be offset by a range of measures that a more active form of economic policy would introduce once the UK became independent. Examples could include the development of innovation and R&D tax credits, active labour market policies to enhance the skill development of specific sectors of the economy and the management of the exchange rate as to ensure the continued competitiveness of UK exporters.

Given the fact that the WTO option maximises the policy flexibility that could be utilised by UK policy makers following the completion of Brexit, it is as compatible as the FTA option with the type of active government required to deal with the long standing problems inherent in the UK economy. Thus, the final judgement concerning the advisability of this scenario depends upon a careful consideration of *both costs and benefits* of this approach, rather than simply the former.

4

What Does the Economics Evidence Tell Us?

In outlining the main options for a future trade relationship between the UK and the EU, it is clear that all have a range of advantages and disadvantages. The choice is therefore complex.[1] This is just the sort of area where economists try to assist policy makers to make decisions by creating an economic model which attempts to predict the relative merits amongst a number of options. The analysis of Brexit options is no exception, as it has generated a large number of studies, using a range of methodologies and producing a quite diverse range of forecasts (Whyman and Petrescu, 2017:35-40).

You might, however, be forgiven for not realising the range of views held by different teams of economists. Most of the attention, given by press and politicians alike, has focused around a small group of studies conducted by such organisations as the London School of Economics (LSE), HM Treasury, OECD, IMF and the National Institute of Economic and Social Research (NIESR). These have tended to use similar approaches to produce their forecasts which, perhaps not surprisingly, generated broadly comparable results. Their significance has been further magnified because other organisations, such as the CBI, the TUC and the Office for Budget Responsibility (OBR), preferred to use their calculations were subsequently used as the basis for later reports produced by the rather than their producing their own independent analysis.

The forecasts produced by these five studies suggested that there would be a smaller negative impact the closer the trade relationship the UK was able to negotiate with the EU, and a larger cost associated with looser trade relationships. The estimates of net costs varied from 1.3% GDP in the most advantageous case, predicted by the LSE and IMF, to a cost of around 7.5% of GDP as forecast by the Treasury and NIESR under their worst case scenario. The EEA was the least-costly scenario, followed by FTAs and finally trading under WTO rules. None of these studies thought to test the impact of a customs union.

If these economic estimates were to be taken at face value, this would provide a strong argument for UK policy makers to push for the closest accommodation with the EU – either seeking EEA membership or through the negotiation of a customs union. There are, however, two significant problems with relying too heavily upon their conclusions.

The first arises from the fact that all studies seeking to predict future behaviour reply upon a range of simplifying assumptions concerning how the economy is supposed to work and how people and organisations are likely to react to different stimuli. Otherwise, the mathematics becomes frighteningly complex. However, to the extent that these assumptions fail to reflect the real world, these models contain inbuilt inaccuracies within their very DNA. Unfortunately, this was the case for all of these five highly cited studies. They drew their inspiration from the same narrow orthodox range of schools of thought within economics (New Keynesian-New Monetarist) whose approximation to the real world is questionable. As a result, they tend to over-emphasise such factors as the importance of migration as a driver of growth, and downplay other factors such as the ability of economic policy intervention to influence expectations and hence the real economy.

The second problem with these studies is perhaps more concerning as it relates to not only what the models contain but, more especially, what they omit. In economics terminology, the models suffer from missing variable bias which significantly skewed their findings.

If we started with a blank sheet of paper, and sought to include as many variables as might be reasonably expected to be impacted by Brexit, we might come up with a list including both factors likely to be either negatively or positively impacted by Brexit. The former may include trade with the EU, inward FDI from the EU, the quantity of net migration and the level of uncertainty arising from Brexit. Whereas benefits arising from Brexit are more likely to be captured through the greater potential for increasing trade with the rest of the world, inward FDI from outside Europe, outward FDI, quality or productivity effects from targeted migration, the cost of regulation, exchange rate changes leading to greater competitiveness and government policy actions.

Perhaps surprisingly, given the reputation of these institutions, the five mainstream studies focused almost exclusively upon the variables from the first list and excluded most of those from the second. As a result, their predictions over-estimated likely costs and under-estimated likely benefits.

By focusing almost entirely upon the problem of what the UK is likely to lose, rather than what it might gain, from having a looser trading relationship with the EU, these studies were almost bound to deliver negative predictions for Brexit as a whole. That is why they advocate EEA over FTA and WTO options. Had the question been framed more broadly, taking into account the UK taking advantage of Brexit to form closer economic and trading relationships with other nations, and using the greater independence from EU regulations to seek to transform its own economy, then these models might have produced very different results.

This can be partly seen in a later study, completed by economists from Cambridge, who varied some of the theoretical assumptions on which the mainstream studies based their calculations. This produced much smaller estimates of net cost of around 1.5% of UK GDP.[2] Had this study also included all of the missing variables, it would be likely to have produced an even more favourable result.

Whilst this sort of disagreement between economists from markedly different schools of thought might seem esoteric and of no great interest to most people, the predictions made concerning Brexit do matter. They set the tone of the debate.

Too many commentators are not sufficiently cautious in their interpretation of what these studies are really demonstrating. It is too easy to overlook the flaws in these models and report their findings more as objective facts – i.e. forecasts showing what *will* happen and not the best estimate of what might happen based upon a range of simplifying assumptions and assuming that key factors (such as government policy) will not change as a result. Firms delay investment because they are concerned about the negative predictions made by the highly cited models. Politicians become confused over the interpretation of the available evidence. As a result, no-one is well served.

Policy makers need a better range of economic studies on which to base their considerations. These need to include *all* of the relevant factors which are likely to have an impact upon the predicted outcomes of different choices. They also need to model the potential benefit to the UK economy from expanding trade with the rest of the world.

In essence, they need to provide more of a balanced score card – one that takes into account what might be gained from expanding economic cooperation with the rest of the world and introducing a different economic policy at home, rather than focusing too heavily upon what might be lost in relation to trade with the EU.

The absence of up to date and more rigorous studies increases the difficulty for policy makers seeking to design appropriate reactions to manage the Brexit process, and for companies seeking to decide when or where to make investments. Indeed, the danger is that forecasts can themselves become self-fulfilling prophesies, as individual businesspeople or consumers react to predicted events and by their changed actions precipitate these same predicted outcomes.

Trade Off: Policy Independence v Sustaining Existing Trade Links

If the current range of economic studies cannot currently provide sufficiently reliable evidence to inform the decision facing policy makers over which version of Brexit to choose, perhaps a different way of examining the issue is to consider the nature of the trade-off between competing objectives.

In an ideal world, where we may indeed simultaneously 'have our cake and eat it', it may be possible to deliver the 'exact the same benefits' as full EU membership whilst simultaneously rediscovering the benefits freed from the constraints imposed by the rules of such membership. This, at least, would appear to be the stated aim of key figures from both main political parties.[3]

The problem with this suggestion is that it is virtually inconceivable that this criteria could ever be met. There will almost inevitably be some kind of trade-off between closer access to EU markets and the enhanced options that greater policy autonomy will deliver. This trade-off is illustrated in Figure 4, where the nature of the choice facing UK politicians can be clearly seen.

Do they, for example, choose to pursue a future relationship with the EU that is as close as possible to current full membership? This would minimise short term trade disruption, but at the cost of trading this off for the opportunity to forge new relationships with the rest of the world and reconfigure economic policy here at home to rebalance and rebuild the domestic economy?

Or do they choose a more independent trading position? This would maximise potential medium and longer term gains, but at the cost of increased short term increases in the cost of trading with the EU?

Or, to try and put this more generally, do our political leaders choose a type of Brexit which leaves things largely unchanged from the status quo, or do they choose a different option which seeks to do things differently?

In this admittedly simplified dichotomy, the EEA (single market) and customs union approaches would fall into the former category, whereas the FTA and WTO options would allow more independent policy approaches.

Clearly, this is only a real choice if the alternatives can indeed deliver realisable benefits that would not be available should EEA or customs union approaches be adopted.

There is, for example, a branch of economics which has adopted the position that government policy is essentially ineffective, as rational individuals anticipate government actions and thereby nullify its effects. Holders of this perspective may, therefore, see little benefit in choosing a Brexit option that provides more scope for government action to rejuvenate the UK economy, because they would believe that this was doomed to inevitable failure.

This is not the position that I would take. Nor, I would presume, would the vast majority of parliamentarians or policy makers in other institutions such as the Bank of England, or else they would have chosen to follow what they would themselves regard as an essentially fruitless occupation. Moreover, having just lived through an economic crisis which has clearly demonstrated the difference that economic policy can make – both when governments get it wrong and when they make more sensible choices – it seems clear to me the great potential that policy interventions can make *if implemented correctly and designed based upon the evidence.*

As a result, I would suggest that, boiled down to basics, the choice that we all have to make is whether we would prefer Brexit to mean:

1. making as fewer changes as possible, because we are pretty happy with the status quo; or whether,

2. we would like to do things differently and therefore need the greater policy independence that is necessary to make these changes.

5

What are the Best Options to Deliver a Progressive Brexit?

Thus far, this pamphlet has sought to do two things. Firstly, it has outlined the various options around which a bespoke deal between the UK and the EU can be negotiated. Too often, these options are repeated in the media debate without ever really explaining what they mean in practice. Hopefully, the arguments outlined here provide a little more clarity. Secondly, I have sought to outline a new economic approach which would meet the more significant economic challenges faced by the UK and, in so doing, produce a progressive form of Brexit – one that delivers benefits for the many and not just the few.

This final section, therefore, seeks to bring both of these parts of the discussion together, in asking which of the various Brexit options has the greatest potential in delivering this agenda. This choice depends crucially upon the answer to the question set earlier – i.e. should the UK choose to keep things largely the same, or to do things differently.

Given the magnitude of the economic challenges facing the UK, and the proposed new economic approach required to address these problems, the necessity to facilitate the transformation of the UK economy has to have a major influence on which Brexit option should be preferred. This should be one which can both maintain as much of existing trade patterns and cooperation with the EU as possible, yet giving policy makers the additional policy instruments and flexibility necessary to deal effectively with the profound economic challenges facing the UK.

The EEA and Customs Union alternatives would do one of these things but not the other, whereas the WTO option would provide more policy independence but at the cost of tariffs on EU trade. To take a Goldilocks analogy – the EEA and Customs Union options would seem too hot, whilst the WTO alternative too cold.

On balance, therefore, the negotiation of a comprehensive Free Trade Agreement (FTA) with the EU would seem to be 'just right' in terms of the balance between maintaining a sizeable proportion of current preferential trade flows whilst providing government with the greater range of policy tools necessary to make the most of the opportunities arising from Brexit.

Is a FTA the Only Way to Get Policy Flexibility?

Critics of this conclusion may dispute the conclusion that a FTA is the best way of delivering the policy flexibility that I have suggested forms the essential feature of how to deliver the most favourable and progressive form of Brexit. Indeed, they might very reasonably argue that the UK does not make the most of those economic policy tools that are currently available to it despite the restrictions imposed by EU membership.

This is undoubtedly true. Successive UK governments have preferred to base their economic strategies upon relatively orthodox economic foundations. Even New Labour, whilst being radical at the margin with the introduction of the National Minimum Wage, tax credits and channelling resources to hard pressed public services, adopted a macroeconomic approach that was very largely based upon neo-liberal principles. Moreover, there is nothing in EU law to prevent future UK governments from embracing a post-Keynesian macroeconomic strategy, of the type I propose.

And, to be clear, because of the UK's opt-out from the rules surrounding the Eurozone single currency, there is nothing preventing the UK from immediately abandoning fiscal austerity irrespective of whether it remains a full member of the EU or not. If the UK did not possess the opt-out, it would be a different story, as the rules of the Stability and Growth Pact would prevent effective counter-cyclical macroeconomic management. But, with the opt-out in place, the UK does preserve a degree more freedom in fiscal policy strategy than Eurozone members.

It is, however, not so clear cut with other aspects of the Left Brexit economic approach. It is the case that a form of horizontal industrial policy is allowed under current EU rules, and that the UK typically has preferred not to use the options which have been available. Indeed, the UK government White Paper concedes this point, when it states proudly that the UK has been amongst the lowest users of state aid as a share of national income in the EU – 0.3% of GDP as compared to the EU average of 0.7% (HMG, 2018:38).

What is *not* correct, however, is to conclude that the UK would be equally as free to develop and use industrial policy measures under whatever form of relationship it wishes to have with the EU – whether the EEA, customs union or indeed to remain a full member of the organisation.

As previously discussed in the section dedicated to industrial policy, current EU competition rules are part of the single market and therefore would form part of the EEA. They are also likely to form part of any customs union agreement, if this follows the Turkish precedent. In order to promote a single European market, these rules seek to prevent state aid or assistance from disproportionately benefitting a firm or a group of firms. This would make it more difficult for UK industrial policy to favour UK producers without the same benefits being available to other producers across the EU. To do so would quickly drain the available resource being channelled into this initiative and it would be less effective in rebuilding domestic capacity.

It is a similar story with public procurement – i.e. where public services purchase goods and services. Under EU rules, all public contracts, irrespective of their size, must be open to all firms from across all EU member states. All tendering details have to be published on the EU's tendering portal (SIMAP). For larger contracts, there are tighter rules and there are different minimum thresholds for different categories of procurement. But generally speaking, anything over around £198,000 is likely to have to adhere to stricter EU rules.[1] Once again, the intent is to protect the integrity of the single market.

In the process, however, the EU rules make it more difficult to use procurement as a means of favouring a nation's own industrial development or awarding contracts to local producers. This would be viewed as discriminatory. Yet, awarding contracts to supply food to schools and hospitals from local famers would have nutrition and environmental (lower food miles) benefits, in addition to boosting local economies. Similarly, EU procurement rules blunt strategies employed by Local Economic Partnerships (LEPs) and local authorities, which attempt to use anchor institutions as a means of retaining a greater proportion of income generated in the local economy, and thereby benefitting from local multiplier (knock-on) effects. The oft-discussed

'Preston Model'[2] and other similar initiatives would be more effective if released from EU procurement rules.

Other aspects of post-Brexit strategy would have a similarly enhanced degree of freedom of manoeuvre. The replacement of EU with national business regulation would likely have a beneficial effect. This need not be through liberalisation, but simply through the process of introducing approaches specifically tailored to meet the needs of a particular economy rather than adhering to rules devised to be applicable across multiple jurisdictions (Whyman and Petrescu, 2017:176-180). Active labour market approaches aimed at targeting skills development in certain groups would be aided by the ability to better control parameters of labour supply. Moreover, the ability for the UK to set financial regulations in the best interests of the real economy, and have the power to control excessive and volatile flows of capital should the need arise, would all be enhanced outside of the requirements of the EEA and its insistence on the 'four freedoms'.

Thus, whilst it is correct to note that the UK does indeed have greater flexibility of action than it typically decides to use, both within full EU membership and alternative EEA and customs union alternatives, the fact that these would require the UK to abide by a set of competition, state aid and procurement rules, would unnecessarily bind the hands of UK governments. It is for this fact, therefore, that a FTA offers a better alternative. It allows greater policy freedom. It provides the ability to develop and enact active policy measures aimed at transforming the UK economy, rather than trying to bend EU rules to achieve a fraction of what would otherwise be possible. It also has the advantage that the UK would not contribute towards EU coffers – under the EEA and customs union approaches, it would be expected to do so.

Given the potential of what could be achieved through the development of a more active economic policy framework, of the type I have described, the advantages of pursuing a FTA rather than other potential Brexit options seems to me to be the logical conclusion.

What Sort of FTA Would Work Best?

The deal completed between the EU and Canada (CETA) demonstrates that a FTA can encompass not only trade in goods but also key areas of services. Since this is a particular specialism for the UK, building on this aspect of a FTA would be advantageous. Given that the UK is starting from regulatory harmonisation with the EU, this should be more straightforward to deliver. However, as discussed earlier, the CETA treaty is not helpful in other aspects, such as its standards on the protection of foreign investors.

As a result, there are two more acceptable forms of FTA that could be sought by the UK. The first option is to propose what should be a relatively straightforward shallower form of FTA. This would focus more narrowly upon free trade in goods and services, whilst largely ignoring deeper aspects such as the introduction of investor-state dispute procedures. This is the simplest form of FTA and should, therefore, be the easiest to negotiate and quickest to implement.

Alternatively, the UK could propose a deeper form of FTA to the EU negotiators, but in a form which sought to limit potential flaws in the CETA approach. Thus, for example, it could seek to ensure that any discussion of investor rights precluded the ability of large trans-national corporations from litigating against the introduction of new policy initiatives by democratic governments. It could also seek to strengthen the enforcement of the labour standards which were included in the CETA treaty. Given the criticism levelled at the design of CETA by the ETUC and various other groups within the EU, the suggestion to incorporate more progressive elements into a trade treaty should be attractive to many across the EU as well as those on the Left in the UK.

My own preference would be for the UK to begin with a shallow form of FTA, which could be more easily negotiated within the current Brexit timetable when combined with the proposed transition agreement. This should embrace all goods and as many services as possible. Since the UK has a competitive advantage in many different types of services, it would be helpful to seek mutual recognition of qualifications and mutual recognition of similar (but not identical) regulations and standards. This shallow FTA could always be deepened over time, as the post-Brexit relationship with the EU and other countries develops.

Once a progressive Brexit strategy has been agreed, it would be advantageous to the negotiations if the aims of the approach were discussed more widely and openly with the UK public. The foundation principles of these negotiations should constantly keep in mind the objective of ensuring that benefits from the new economic strategy are experienced across the whole of the UK. There should be no 'left behind' areas that do not share in the economic developments that follow Brexit. It would help the UK negotiators in there was a sense that the country was broadly supportive of the overall approach.

Prepare for a No Deal, Negotiate for a Better Deal
It is also important that the UK should accelerate its preparations for a post-Brexit future. This is for two main reasons.

The first is that it strengthens the hand of the UK

negotiating team. Anyone who has taken part in a negotiation knows that the UK position is weakened by any failure to demonstrate that there is a viable alternative to accepting whatever the negotiations deliver. Otherwise, the temptation will be for the EU to seek ever increasing concessions. Therefore, to deliver a mutually beneficial (not a one-sided) agreement, the UK threat that it could walk away from the negotiating table has to be seen as credible. And it will not unless preparations have already been made for this 'plan B' scenario.

The second reason is that, either because of miscalculation or an unwillingness to find a mutually beneficial compromise solution, negotiations with the EU over a suitable FTA might fail. The former Greek finance minister, Yanis Varoufakis, has been quite consistent in his view that the EU bureaucracy will wish to frustrate the negotiation of a mutually beneficial agreement in order to protect the stability of the European project.[3] Whether he is correct in his assessment or not, the failure to reach a mutually advantageous agreement would result in the UK either having to accept an unsuitable 'take it or leave it' deal, which could compromise the future success of its economy, or opt to trade under WTO rules unless or until it was possible to reach a suitable trade deal.

It would be an act of folly if the UK were forced into a position where it felt that it had to lock its future into an arrangement which imposed additional costs upon the UK economy but imposed constraints upon the ability of the country to benefit from the new opportunities that a progressive Brexit solution would offer. No deal, in this sense, is always better than a bad deal. But, of course, this does not have to be the end point in discussions – it could simply be round one in a longer duration realignment of cooperation between the UK, the EU and other nations.

As a result, the UK needs to hasten its practical planning for life as an independent nation after Brexit is completed. This would include making faster progress in finalising new customs arrangements to manage trade between the UK and the EU which potentially may occur outside of current customs union arrangement. In the short term, this is most easily achieved by expanding the existing Customs Handling of Import and Export Freight (CHIEF) system that currently manages UK trade with the rest of the world. In the medium term, upgrading to a smarter borders approach should be gradually introduced and therefore the development and testing of the technology and software systems should begin in order for this to be rolled out in a once this has been satisfactorily completed.

Government should also accelerate work being undertaken by the Migration Advisory Committee with regard to designing a new migration approach and to identify those areas where replacing EU with national regulation could more effectively meet the challenges faced by UK businesses. Consultation with all affected stakeholders – employers and trade unions – should hopefully mitigate unforeseen consequences in any and all of these proposals.

To further strengthen the negotiators hand, it would be advantageous if the UK were to demonstrate popular support for its negotiating position. That would be far easier to achieve if that was in turn based upon a progressive and inclusive version of Brexit – one where the benefits of the new economic approach are shared as widely as possible throughout the whole of the UK.

This requires a commitment, from government, that both the short term costs and longer term benefits arising from Brexit will be shared by all communities across the UK, and not concentrated in a few privileged hands.

This will help to ensure that this time we really are all in it together.

Proposals on how to use a more active form of both industrial and labour market policies need to be developed and shared with the citizens of the UK, in rather the same way that the Beveridge reforms gave hope and confidence to an anxious population well in advance of actual implementation. Public procurement should be re-imagined to assist in the rejuvenation of the UK productive base, and to help local communities to anchor economic prosperity within their own regions. A more active (post-Keynesian) macroeconomic policy stance should be developed to further facilitate this new policy framework.

Conclusion

As I have hopefully shown, it is entirely possible, indeed necessary, for a sustainable Brexit solution to be both outward looking and progressive. To promote high quality jobs and the reinvigoration of the UK economy. To spread the benefits of future prosperity across the whole of the UK – ensuring that all communities across the UK share fairly in future prosperity once the Brexit process has been completed. A Left Brexit must ensure that the transformation of the economy benefits the many and not just the few.

The motivation behind writing this pamphlet has been to show how this progressive form of Brexit can make a positive difference to our nation. But its success crucially depends upon two things.

Firstly, that the choice of post-Brexit relationship with the EU is sufficiently flexible to allow sufficient changes in economic policies in order to be able to deliver a successful Brexit outcome. For the reasons outlined earlier, the best solution would be a free trade agreement (FTA) which avoids having to tie the UK economy too closely to the EU's rules and regulations. This is a necessary but not, by itself, sufficient condition to secure a progressive Brexit solution.

Secondly, the success of a progressive form of Brexit requires all of us to press for a fairer, more inclusive set of policies that will ensure that the UK emerges from withdrawal more confident in itself and more capable of meeting the challenges and opportunities of the future. It requires our politicians to embrace the essential elements of this approach and get on with planning our post-Brexit future. And our EU partners to negotiate in good faith for a deal that benefits everyone concerned.

The sooner we start, the sooner the benefits of a progressive Brexit can begin to materialise.

References

Anson, J., Cadot, O., Estevadeordal, A., de Melo, J., Suwa-Eisenmann, A. and Tumurchudur, B. (2004), 'Rules of Origin in North-South Preferential Trading Arrangements with an Application to NAFTA', *Research Unit Working Paper* No. 0406, Laboratoire d'Economie Appliquee, INRA, Paris.

Balaram, B., Warden, J. and Wallace-Stephens, F. (2017), *Good Gigs: A fairer future for the UK's gig economy*, Royal Society for the Encouragement of Arts, Manufactures and Connerce (RSA), London. Available via: https://www.thersa.org/globalassets/pdfs/reports/rsa_good-gigs-fairer-gig-economy-report.pdf.

Bank of England (2015), *EU Membership and the Bank of England*, Bank of England, London. Available via: http://www.bankofengland.co.uk/publications/Documents/speeches/2015/euboe211015.pdf.

Bohanes, J. (2015), WTO *Dispute Settlement and Industrial Policy: E15 Expert Group on Reinvigorating Manufacturing*, International Centre for Trade and Sustainable Development (ICTSD) and World Economic Forum, Geneva. Available via: http://e15initiative.org/wp-content/uploads/2015/09/E15-Industrial-Policy-Bohanes-FINAL.pdf.

Carrere, C. and De Melo, J. (2004), 'Are Different Rules of Origin Equally Costly? Estimates from NAFTA', *CEPR Discussion Paper* No. 4437, CEPR, London.

CBI [Confederation of British Industry] (2013), *Our Global Future: The Business Vision for a Reformed EU*, CBI, London. Available via: http://www.cbi.org.uk/media/2451423/our_global_future.pdf#page=1&zoom=auto,-119,842.

CBI [Confederation of British Industry] (2016), *Leaving the EU: Implications for the UK economy*, PwC Report. Available via: http://www.cbi.org.uk/news/leaving-eu-would-cause-a-serious-shock-to-uk-economy-new-pwc-analysis/leaving-the-eu-implications-for-the-uk-economy/.

Chisik, R. (2003), 'Export Industry Policy and Reputational Comparative Advantage', *Journal of International Economics*, 59(2): 423-451.

Conservative Party (2017), *Forward Together: Our Plan for a Stronger Britain and a Prosperous Future – The Conservative and Unionist Party Manifesto 2017*, Conservative party, London. Available via: https://www.conservatives.com/manifesto.

Dinnie, K. (2008), *Nation Branding: Concepts, issues, practice*, Routledge, Abingdon.

Dustmann, C. and Frattini, T. (2014), 'The Fiscal Effects of Immigration to the UK', *Economic Journal*, 124: F595-F643.

EU [European Union] (2010), *Consolidated Treaties: The Treaty on European Union and The Treaty on the Functioning of the European Union*, Publications Office of the European Union, Luxembourg.

Guest, D.E. and Peccei, R. (2001), 'Partnership at Work: Mutuality and the Balance of Advantage', *British Journal of Industrial Relations*, 39(2): 207–236.

HMG [Her Majesty's Government] (2017), *Future Customs Arrangements: A future partnership paper*, The Stationary Office, London. Available via: https://assets.publishing.service.gov.uk/government/uploads/system/uploads/attachment_data/file/637748/Future_customs_arrangements_-_a_future_partnership_paper.pdf.

HMG [Her Majesty's Government] (2018), *The Future Relationship Between the United Kingdom and the European Union*, The Stationary Office, London. Available via: https://assets.publishing.service.gov.uk/government/uploads/system/uploads/attachment_data/file/725288/The_future_relationship_between_the_United_Kingdom_and_the_European_Union.pdf.

Holmes, P. and Jacob, N. (2018), 'Certificates and Rules of Origin: The Experience of UK Firms', *UK Trade Observatory Briefing Paper* No. 15. Available via: http://blogs.sussex.ac.uk/uktpo/files/2018/01/BP15-CRoO.pdf.

Hui, M.K. and Zhou, L. (2002), 'Linking Product Evaluations and Purchase Intention for Country-of-Origin Effects', *Journal of Global Marketing*, 15(3/4): 95-116.

IMF (2016), *IMF Direction of Trade Statistics 2016*, IMF, Washington DC. Available via: www.data.imf.org.

IMF (2018), *World Economic Outlook*, IMF, Washington DC, April.

Karlsson, L. (2017), *Smart Border 2.0: Avoiding a hard border on the island of Ireland for customs control and the free movement of persons*, Policy Department for Citizens' Rights and Constitutional Affairs, European Parliament, Brissels. Available via: http://www.europarl.europa.eu/RegData/etudes/STUD/2017/596828/IPOL_STU(2017)596828_EN.pdf.

Krugman, P. (1994), *The Age of Diminished Expectations*, MIT Press, Cambridge, Ma.

Labour Party (2017), *Where We Stand: Our Manifesto – For the Many, Not the Few*, Labour Party, London. Available via: https://labour.org.uk/manifesto/.

Lepanjuuri, K. Wishart, R. and Cornick, P. (2018), The Characteristics of those in the Gig Economy – Final report, Department for Business, Energy and Industrial Strategy (BEIS), London. Available via: https://assets.publishing.service.gov.uk/government/uploads/system/uploads/attachment_data/file/687553/The_characteristics_of_those_in_the_gig_economy.pdf.

Lowe, S. (2018), *Brexit and Rule of Origin: Why Free Trade Agreements ≠ Free Trade*, Centre for European Reform, London. Available via: http://www.cer.eu/insights/brexit-and-rules-origin-why-free-trade-agreements-≠-free-trade.

Manyika, J., Lund, S., Bughin, J., Robinson, K., Mischke, J. and Mahajan, D. (2016), *Independent Work: Choice, necessity and the gig economy*, McKinsey Global Institute, New York and London. Available via: https://www.mckinsey.com/~/media/McKinsey/Global%20Themes/Employment%20and%20Growth/Independent%20work%20Choice%20necessity%20and%20the%20gig%20economy/Independent-Work-Choice-necessity-and-the-gig-economy-Executive-Summary.ashx.

Michie, J., and Sheehan-Quinn, M. (2001), 'Labour Market Flexibility, Human Resource Management and Corporate Performance,' *British Journal of Management*, 12, 287–306.

Miller, M. and Spencer, J. (1977), 'The Static Economic Effects of the UK Joining the EEC: A General Equilibrium Approach', *Review of Economic Studies*, 44(1): 71–93.

Newsome, K., Heyes, J., Moore, S., Smith, D. and Tomlinson, M. (2018), *Living on the Edge: Experiencing workplace insecurity in the UK*, Trades Union Congress (TUC), London. Available via: https://www.tuc.org.uk/living-edge.

NOU [Official Norwegian Report] (2012a), *Utenfor og Innenfor:*

Norges avtaler med EU [Outside and Inside: Norway's agreement's with the EU], NOU 2012:2, Norwegian Ministry of Foreign Affairs, Oslo. Available via: https://www.regjeringen.no/contentassets/5d3982d042a2472eb1b20639cd8b2341/no/pdfs/nou201220120002000dddpdfs.pdf.

NOU [Official Norwegian Report] (2012b), *Outside and Inside: Norway's agreements with the European Union – Other Parties' Views on Norway's Agreements with the EU* – Chapter 13, NOU 2012:2, Norwegian Ministry of Foreign Affairs, Oslo. Available via: http://www.eu-norway.org/Global/SiteFolders/webeu/NOU2012_2_Chapter%2013.pdf.

OECD [Organisation for Economic Cooperation and Development] (2018), *GDP per hour worked*. Available from: http://stats.oecd.org/Index.aspx?DataSetCode=PDB_LV.

ONS [Office of National Statistics] (2017), National Archives, Available via: http://webarchive.nationalarchives.gov.uk/20160105160709/http://www.ons.gov.uk/ons/publications/re-reference-tables.html?edition=tcm%3A77-392545.

Open Britain (2018), *Busting the Lexit Myths*, Open Britain / Labour Campaign for the Single Market, London. Available via: https://d3n8a8pro7vhmx.cloudfront.net/in/pages/14074/attachments/original/1517224151/lexit_paper_finalONLINE.pdf?1517224151.

Portes, J. (2013), 'Commentary: The economic implications for the UK of leaving the European Union', *National Institute Economic Review*, No. 266, F4-9. Available via: http://www.niesr.ac.uk/sites/default/files/commentary.pdf.

Siebert. H. (1997), 'Labor Market Rigidities: At the Root of Unemployment in Europe', *Journal of Economic Perspectives*, 11(3): 37-54.

Sterling, A. and King, L. (2017), *Financing Investment: Reforming finance markets for the long-term*, Institute for Public Policy Research (IPPR), London. Available via: https://www.ippr.org/files/2017-11/cej-finance-and-investment-discussion-paper-a4-report-17-07-21.pdf.

Takyi, D. and D'Silva, E. (2017), *The Impact of Sterling Depreciation on Prices and Turnover in the UK Manufacturing Sector, 2017*, Office for National Statistics, London. Available via: https://www.ons.gov.uk/economy/inflationandpriceindices/articles/theimpactofsterlingdevaluationonpricesandturnoverinthemanufacturingsector/2017-09-15.

Vargas-Silva, C. (2016), *The Fiscal Impact of Immigration in the UK*, Migration Observatory, Oxford. Available via: http://migrationobservatory.ox.ac.uk/wp-content/uploads/2016/04/Briefing-Fiscal_Impacts.pdf.

Viner, J. (1950), *The Customs Union Issue*, Oxford University Press, Oxford, 2014 edition.

Whyman, P.B. (2006), 'British Trade Unions and EMU: Natural supporters or conflicting interests?', in Whyman, P.B., Baimbridge, M. and Burkitt, B. (eds.), *Implications of the Euro: A Critical Perspective from the Left*, Routledge, Abingdon, 137-144.

Whyman, P.B. (2018), 'Breixt: A Cliff Edge or a Small Bump in the Road?', *Political Quarterly*, 89(2): 298-305.

Whyman, P.B. and Petrescu, A.I. (2014), 'Partnership, Flexible Workplace Practices and the Realisation of Mutual Gains: Evidence from the British WERS 2004 dataset', *International Journal of Human Resource Management*, 25(6): 829-851.

Whyman, P.B. and Petrescu, A.I. (2017), *The Economics of Brexit: A Cost-Benefit Analysis of the UK's Economic Relationship with the EU*, Palgrave, Basingstoke.

Whyman, P.B., Baimbridge, M. and Mullen, A. (2012), *The Political Economy of the European Social Model*, Routledge, Abingdon.

World Bank (2005), Global Economic Prospects, IBRD / World Bank, Washington DC. Available via: http://siteresources.worldbank.org/INTGEP2005/Resources/gep2005.pdf.

World Bank (2016), *Gross Capital Formation Report*. Available via: http://databank.worldbank.org/data/reports.aspx?source=2&series=NE.GDI.TOTL.ZS&country=#

WTO [World Trade Organisation] (2011), *World Trade Report: The WTO and Preferential Trade Agreements*, WTO, Geneva.

Notes

Abbreviations

1 https://www.economist.com/the-economist-explains/2015/08/24/
   why-the-schengen-agreement-might-be-under-threat; http://www.
   cer.eu/in-the-press/schengen-2018

Introduction

1 The contradictions between social Europe and the requirements of
   the single currency in the EU is discussed by Whyman (2006) and
   Whyman et al (2012). The full text of the Delors speech to the TUC
   can be found at http://www.open.edu/openlearn/ocw/pluginfile.
   php/614790/mod_resource/content/1/ReadingsEF.pdf.

2. Creating a Resilient Economy

1 http://researchbriefings.parliament.uk/ResearchBriefing/Summary/
   SN02815#fullreport.

2 https://www.ons.gov.uk/economy/nationalaccounts/
   balanceofpayments/bulletins/uktrade/january2018.

3 https://www.theguardian.com/business/2018/apr/08/why-the-uk-
   trade-deficit-with-the-eu-is-woeful-and-widening.

4 https://www.ons.gov.uk/employmentandlabourmarket/
   peopleinwork/labourproductivity/bulletins/labourproductivity/
   jantomar2016

5 https://data.worldbank.org/indicator/NE.GDI.FTOT.
   KD.ZG?end=2016&start=2016; OECD (2016).

6 As a technical note, according to the World Bank this is gross capital
   formation, not gross fixed capital formation; the difference being
   that Gross capital formation consists of outlays on additions to

fixed assets (i.e. land improvements, plant, machinery and other equipment purchases, together with the improvement of physical infrastructure such as roads, railways, buildings, schools and hospitals), and the net change in inventories.

7 https://www.ft.com/content/83e7e87e-fe64-11e6-96f8-3700c5664d30; https://www.independent.co.uk/news/business/news/uk-workers-have-had-the-worst-wage-growth-in-the-oecd-except-greece-a7773246.html.

8 https://www.theguardian.com/commentisfree/2017/sep/03/employment-rights-risk-brexit-eu-withdrawal-bill; https://www.ft.com/content/8d5dbf2e-f20f-11e7-ac08-07c3086a2625; https://www.tuc.org.uk/blogs/revealed-right-wing-plans-scrap-workers-rights-after-brexit.

9 https://assets.publishing.service.gov.uk/government/uploads/system/uploads/attachment_data/file/248096/0061.pdf; https://www.gov.uk/government/speeches/chancellor-george-osbornes-budget-2014-speech

10 https://www.gov.uk/government/news/2011-budget-britain-open-for-business; https://www.gov.uk/government/speeches/chancellor-we-need-a-northern-powerhouse.

11 http://speri.dept.shef.ac.uk/wp-content/uploads/2015/07/Brief14-Has-the-UK-economy-been-rebalanced.pdf.

12 https://www.gov.uk/government/speeches/the-governments-negotiating-objectives-for-exiting-the-eu-pm-speech.

13 https://data.worldbank.org/indicator/NE.GDI.FTOT.KD.ZG?end=2016&start=2016; OECD (2016).

14 Sterling, A. and King, L. (2017), Financing Investment: Reforming finance markets for the long-term, Institute for Public Policy Research (IPPR), London. Available via: https://www.ippr.org/files/2017-11/cej-finance-and-investment-discussion-paper-a4-report-17-07-21.pdf.

15 GATT 1947, Part I, Article I, incorporated into GATT 1994 as Annex 1A to the WTO Agreement 1994; GATT 1947, Part II, Article III, incorporated into GATT 1994 as Annex 1A to the WTO Agreement 1994. See also the WTO Agreement on Subsidies and Countervailing Measures, incorporated into GATT 1994 as part of Annex 1A to the WTO Agreement 1994.

3. Making a Choice – What Type of Brexit?

1 http://www.cer.eu/insights/brexit-and-rules-origin-why-free-trade-
   agreements-≠-free-trade.

2 https://ec.europa.eu/taxation_customs/business/calculation-customs-
   duties/rules-origin/general-aspects-preferential-origin/arrangements-
   list/paneuromediterranean-cumulation-pem-convention_en#pem

3 http://www.stephenkinnock.co.uk/with_the_eea_vote_the_lords_
   can_set_theresa_may_on_the_right_brexit_path.

4 It has been suggested, by Open Europe and elsewhere, that EU rules
   are not an impediment to the future renationalisation of particular
   industries, such as the railways or utility companies (West et al,
   2018:10-13). It is certainly true that many EU member states have
   significant state owned companies. Similarly, EU rules do not
   specifically prevent renationalisation per se. But they do affect the
   type of nationalisation that is possible whilst the UK remains a
   member of the EU, and would equally apply under EEA or customs
   union Brexit options. The EU has a long standing commitment
   to liberalise industries, including the railways, and would insist
   upon continued open access for private firms to be able to use the
   network, and compete against any state owned entity. The same
   would be true for utility companies. Even though these are natural
   monopolies – i.e. where fixed costs are so high that it doesn't make
   economic sense to have multiple firms engaged in this market.
   Thus, the railways could indeed be taken into public hands, but
   the track and operating companies would need to be separate,
   and private operators would have the right to run trains on the
   system, thereby frustrating one of the arguments for bringing the
   railways back together under public ownership, namely the ability to
   properly coordinate the system. There would need to be a tendering
   process, where the state owned operator could compete against
   private companies for the award of a franchise, rather than having
   a national, consolidated system. As a result, EU rules would not
   prevent nationalisation but would certainly prevent this from taking
   a form that would allow greater integration and coordination of
   activities, with the resulting economies of scale.

5 http://ec.europa.eu/trade/policy/countries-and-regions/countries/
   turkey/; https://ec.europa.eu/taxation_customs/business/calculation-
   customs-duties/rules-origin/customs-unions/turkey-customs-unions-
   preferential-arrangements_en

6 https://www.ft.com/content/fbdc5d58-5e97-11e8-9334-2218e7146b04.

7   https://briefingsforbrexit.com/customs-costs-post-brexit-long-version/.

8   http://data.parliament.uk/writtenevidence/committeeevidence.svc/evidencedocument/eu-external-affairs-subcommittee/brexit-customs-arrangements/written/85217.pdf.

9   http://data.parliament.uk/writtenevidence/committeeevidence.svc/evidencedocument/eu-external-affairs-subcommittee/brexit-customs-arrangements/written/85217.pdf.

10   http://data.parliament.uk/writtenevidence/committeeevidence.svc/evidencedocument/eu-external-affairs-subcommittee/brexit-customs-arrangements/oral/84048.pdf.

11   http://data.parliament.uk/writtenevidence/committeeevidence.svc/evidencedocument/eu-external-affairs-subcommittee/brexit-customs-arrangements/written/83040.pdf.

12   https://www.ft.com/content/23111758-4dfc-11e8-8a8e-22951a2d8493.

13   https://www.bloomberg.com/news/articles/2018-07-26/eu-said-to-see-brexit-customs-plan-as-more-magical-thinking.

14   https://www.ft.com/content/aeb53c82-82ac-11e8-96dd-fa565ec55929.

15   https://www.bbc.co.uk/news/uk-politics-44761416.

16   https://www.gov.uk/government/speeches/the-governments-negotiating-objectives-for-exiting-the-eu-pm-speech.

17   https://www.wto.org/english/tratop_e/region_e/region_e.htm

18   https://www.irishtimes.com/news/politics/bertie-ahern-technology-and-turning-blind-eye-could-solve-brexit-border-issue-1.3306710.

19   https://www.bloomberg.com/news/articles/2018-01-08/u-k-should-have-canada-plus-plus-plus-brexit-deal-italy-says.

20   https://corporateeurope.org/sites/default/files/attachments/great-ceta-swindle.pdf.

21   https://www.ictu.ie/download/pdf/no_deal.pdf.

22   https://corporateeurope.org/sites/default/files/attachments/great-ceta-swindle.pdf.

23   https://www.etuc.org/sites/default/files/document/files/07-en-statement_-_etuc_assessment_on_ceta_-_final.pdf.

24   World Bank (2015), MFN (Most Favourite Nation) tariff rate 1988 - 2014. Available via: http://data.worldbank.org/indicator/TM.TAX.MRCH.WM.AR.ZS?locations=EU; World Data Bank (2016), Tariff rate series. World Development Indicators.

25   https://www.wto.org/english/tratop_e/region_e/region_e.htm

4. What Does the Economics Evidence Tell Us?

1 There is a more detailed evaluation of the weaknesses with the most cited mainstream studies given in Whyman and Petrescu (2017).

2 Gudgin, G., Coutts, K. and Gibson, N. (2017), The Macro-economic Impact of Brexit: Using the CBR Macroeconomic model of the UK economy (UKMOD), Centre for Business Research Working Paper No. 483. Available via: http://www.cbr.cam.ac.uk/fileadmin/user_upload/centre-for-business-research/downloads/working-papers/wp483revised.pdf.

3 https://hansard.parliament.uk/commons/2017-01-24/debates/D423AEE6-BE36-4935-AD6A-5CA316582A9C/Article50; https://labourlist.org/2017/03/keir-starmer-labour-has-six-tests-for-brexit-if-theyre-not-met-we-wont-back-the-final-deal-in-parliament/.

5. What are the Best Options to Deliver a Progressive Brexit?

1 https://europa.eu/youreurope/business/public-tenders/rules-procedures/index_en.htm.

2 https://www.theguardian.com/cities/2017/apr/11/preston-cleveland-model-lessons-recovery-rust-belt; https://cles.org.uk/the-preston-model/.

3 http://www.independent.co.uk/news/world/europe/theresa-may-brexit-tactics-wrong-eu-former-greek-finance-minister-yanis-varoufakis-a7721151.html; https://www.ft.com/content/9763be78-5832-11e7-9fed-c19e2700005f.